Spirits of the Water

Jaq D Hawkins

Illustrations by Jeremy Scott

Spirits of the Water

©2000 Jaq D Hawkins

ISBN 186163 0905

ALL RIGHTS RESERVED

No part of this publication may be reproduced, stored in a retrieval system or transmitted in any form or by any means, electronic, mechanical, photocopying, scanning, recording or otherwise without the prior written permission of the author and the publisher.

Cover design by Paul Mason
Cover painitng by Marc Potts

Published by:

Capall Bann Publishing
Freshfields
Chieveley
Berks
RG20 8TF

Acknowledgments

Thanks for this volume are due perhaps mostly to the 'Watery' people I have met in my life, but also to everyone who has ever made me feel anything; Love, hate, joy, rage...because like the actor, the magician can make use of each of these experiences in their work.

Special thanks are due to Kevin as always, both for starting me on the road to this series and for staying my friend through the storms of transition, and especially to Mary Clacy, for all of the contributuions she has made toward the chapter on holy wells, from tours to photographs.

This one is dedicated to my Mother,
who told me repeatedly as a child that no matter
how bad things seem at any given time,
it always works out in the end,
which has always contributed to my eternal optimism.
Also dedicated as always,
to my own daughter, Wendy LeFay,
and to Anton,
for bringing the joy of
insane, chaotic Love into my life.

The Author

Jaq D. Hawkins began magical study as a child and has been aware of elemental spirits from a very young age, despite a primarily urban upbringing. Her writings on various aspects of magical theory are recognized in American as well as British occult magazines and are repeated on various computer networks. Her writings on the relationship of elemental spirits to the natural laws of our world are unique to this series of books. Ms. Hawkins currently lives in the North of England with her daughter and their cat, Lucky.

The Illustrator

Jeremy Scott is a native of North Yorkshire where he attended Harrogate College of Arts. He has sold his artwork in private galleries as well as doing commissioned work, primarily his astoundingly realistic technical drawings. More recently, he has also become known for his striking landscapes. He has diversified his talents into designing theatre sets, illustrating children's books, and has even turned his hand to specialized interior design in San Francisco. His special talent for incorporating elemental creatures into his drawings is a valuable asset to this series. At the time of writing, Mr. Scott is somewhere in India, gone walk-a-bout for six months, but we hope for his return in time to illustrate the final book of the series, and look forward to the visual effects of his spiritual quest.

Also By The Author:

Understanding Chaos Magic
Spirits of the Earth
Spirits of the Air
Spirits of the Fire

Books In Progress;

Spirits of the Aether
The Chaos Monkey

Table of Contents

Introduction to the Spirits of the Elements Series	1
1 The Nature of Water	5
2 Types of Water Spirits	15
3 In the Depths of a Well	31
4 Places to Find Water Spirits	49
5 To See Water Spirits	57
6 Water Spirits In Natural Magic	67
7 Water Spirits In Ritual	75
8 Correspondences	83
9 Water Thought-Form Elementals	91
10 Divination With Water Spirits	99
11 Living With Water Spirits	111
Appendix	115
An Opening For A Water Spirit Ritual	115
Calling A Water Quarter Guardian	116
A Closing For A Water Spirit Ritual	117
The Middle Bit	118
A Spell For Inviting Water Spirits Into The Home Or Temple	118
Inviting A Spirit Into An Object To Represent Water	122
To Charge An Object By Water	123
Evoking A Water Spirit Out Of The Depths	124
To Sustain A Water Spirit	126
Simple Folk Spells And Other Magic	128
Healing With Water Spirits	129
A Fertility Spell	132
A Water Meditation	134
Charging A Driftwood Sigil	135
Cleansing and Purification Spells	136
A Spell To Seek Marriage	137
A Spell To Seek Happiness	138
A Spell To Bring Sleep	141

A Spell To Promote Lucid Dreaming	143
Water Spirit Divinations and	145
A Spell To Assist In Psychic Acts	145
Spawning A Water Thought-Form Elemental	146
Grounding After A Water Spell	149
Bibliography	154

Introduction to the Spirits of the Elements Series

The Spirits of the Elements Series began when a friend of mine who is a palmist told me in a reading that I was destined to write a series of books about nature spirits. At first, I tried to associate this prediction with a series of children's books which I was working on at the time, as it involves characters and events taken directly from my studies about elemental spirits. However, my friend insisted that this was not the series of which he spoke. There would be a series of books written for an adult audience which he was looking forward to reading.

At first, I wondered if the material would have been sufficiently covered by books already in print. However, this concern melted away as the chapters began to form in my mind.

I believe in fairies. Call them what you will, I believe that the spirits of natural things, and some things which would seem at first as not natural, exist whether or not we choose to believe in them. These elemental spirits are very much a part of our world which we cannot afford to ignore or dismiss if we are to understand our own magical nature, or that which draws us into the world of magic.

The four alchemical elements are Earth, Air, Fire and Water. References to these four elements are used in many forms of Paganism and Magic. They represent the material world for

Earth, inspiration for Air, determination for Fire, and emotion for Water. There is a fifth element called Aether. This represents Spirit.

In the following chapters, I will explain the associations and correspondences which humans have attached to the element for this volume, but let's not forget that this is essentially a book about nature spirits. It is their nature that I hope to express in these pages. I also hope to offer some practical information about the methods of perceiving these spirits and perhaps inviting them into the home or into ritual practices. One must remember that these entities cannot be commanded, only invited. I strongly recommend respecting their independence. It is no accident that old tales about fairies often warn of danger, or at least trickery! More about that later.

One quick note for those who wish to see fairies; visual perception is rare but not unknown. They are not physically perceived with the eye in the same way as solid objects. If one studies the medical information learned over many years about how the eye perceives line and colour, one learns that there are receptors in the eyeball called rods and cones. The rods, which are shaped as the name would suggest, perceive line and definition while the cones, which are shaped like little round cones (what a surprise) perceive colour. The combined messages are sent to the brain and we 'see' things as a whole comprising defined shape and colour.

Seeing nature spirits requires a shift in our perception because the rods in our eyes perceive nothing from them. It is the cones which can perceive nature spirits, which is why they are so often depicted as brightly coloured and fanciful little creatures. To an extent, their shape is defined by what we expect it to be. It is also because they are perceived with the cones that they become elusive when one tries to look directly at them. Cones perceive periphially. To see a fairy, one must try to catch it with the corner of one's eye. Perhaps this is at least part of the reason that so many people find it difficult to believe that they were ever there at all...

"And I felt a little bit giddy
Ghostly
As I fished the long pool tail
Peering into that superabundance of spirit."

>Excerpt from *Fishing*,
>by Ted Hughes

1

The Nature of Water

Water is the element of the depths of emotion and of the subconscious. Water rules purification, the unknown, love and the other emotions. Fluid, flowing from one level to another, it is ever changing, yet the changes of Water are very different from the sudden, sometimes devastating changes of Fire. Water can cause sudden devastation in the landscape and in the lives of those who happen to get in the way of a flash flood or a tidal wave. Yet, the nature of the disaster is of a fluid, cleansing sort rather than the destruction of the consumptive power of Fire. In *The Holy Stream*, James Rattue tells us that "*Fire cleanses with violence, but Water with gentleness.*" He also tells us that; "*Water is 'other'.*" and that "*It emerges in a miraculous way from the earth, for it is neither living, nor inanimate; it possesses life, yet is not itself alive, and unlike fire, can never fully be domesticated.*" The power of the raging sea as well as the gentle magic associated with holy wells and the meditative nature of pools and ponds represent the diversity of the nature of Water.

Water is associated with absorption and germination. Pleasure, friendship, marriage, fertility, love, happiness, healing, sleep, dreaming, psychic acts, are all identified with Water, although some of these things may also be approached through other elements. Water is believed to give access to the world of spirits, and many a tale is told of hidden 'ways' to the land of Faery at the bottom of a lake or well.

Water spells are based on the emotions, performed on the intuitive level. Most of all, Water represents intuition. The symbol most often associated with Water is the cup, which holds hidden depths. Within those depths of hidden knowledge lie the secrets of the interrelation of all of the elements, among other things.

Water worship has been widespread throughout civilizations as early as 6000 - 4000 BC, as is evidenced by Water symbols found on goddess and other statues which date from those periods, especially in south-eastern Europe as well as ancient Rome, ancient Egypt, Babylon, Troy and classical Greece. It is also found among aboriginal peoples from Africa, Australia and the Americas.

On a physical level, Water covers 67% of our planet, and encompasses 70% of our body mass. We must have Water to live. We can survive for days or even months without food, but without Water, only a couple of days at best. Water conducts electricity, reverberates sound and absorbs electromagnetic energy. Perhaps this is why some tales tell of certain spirits which cannot cross Water.

Water represents the feminine, as does the Moon. How appropriate then, that the effects of the Moon's gravity are most easily observed in the element of Water; in the tides of the ocean which can also be measured on something as small as a glass of Water and on the mood swings we experience, which can be measured by the records of any police department or mental institution at the time of the Full Moon.

Spiritual meditation is associated with the calm Waters of the soul. Water is generally associated with calm, and indeed will calm itself if left on its own. It is only when one adds other elements, such as winds or earthquakes at sea that Water becomes a raging torrent or wall of destruction. Left to itself, Water sedately breeds life. A pool of Water will develop life and illustrate the cycle of creation and natural putrefaction. Yet the calm pool still reacts to the gravitational tides caused by the Moon. Water reacts to all that occurs around it, reflecting phenomena as our emotions reflect all that occurs in our lives.

It is an old English saying that "*All things begin and end with the sea.*" The sea is one of the most powerful forces in nature, perhaps even the most powerful force on the planet. Indeed, magic itself reacts deeply to the use of powerful emotions. In any form of sea magic, the Moon's phase is particularly important in relation to the rhythm of the tides in the location where the spell is to be performed. Scientists have done experiments with shellfish in which they observed the changes in their natural rhythms when the shellfish were moved from one location to another. In one experiment, a group of mussels were taken to a location in the midwestern United States where there is no ocean, yet the shells opened and closed in rhythm with the times the tides would have occurred had there been an ocean present.

Water is deep and mysterious, and infinitely associated with magic and with elemental spirits. Folklore abounds with Water spirits of various sorts, the most well known perhaps being the Mermaid. These spirits of Water are more often directly associated with magic than those of the other elements. They vary from malicious spirits who entice unwary humans to a Watery death, to benevolent Water

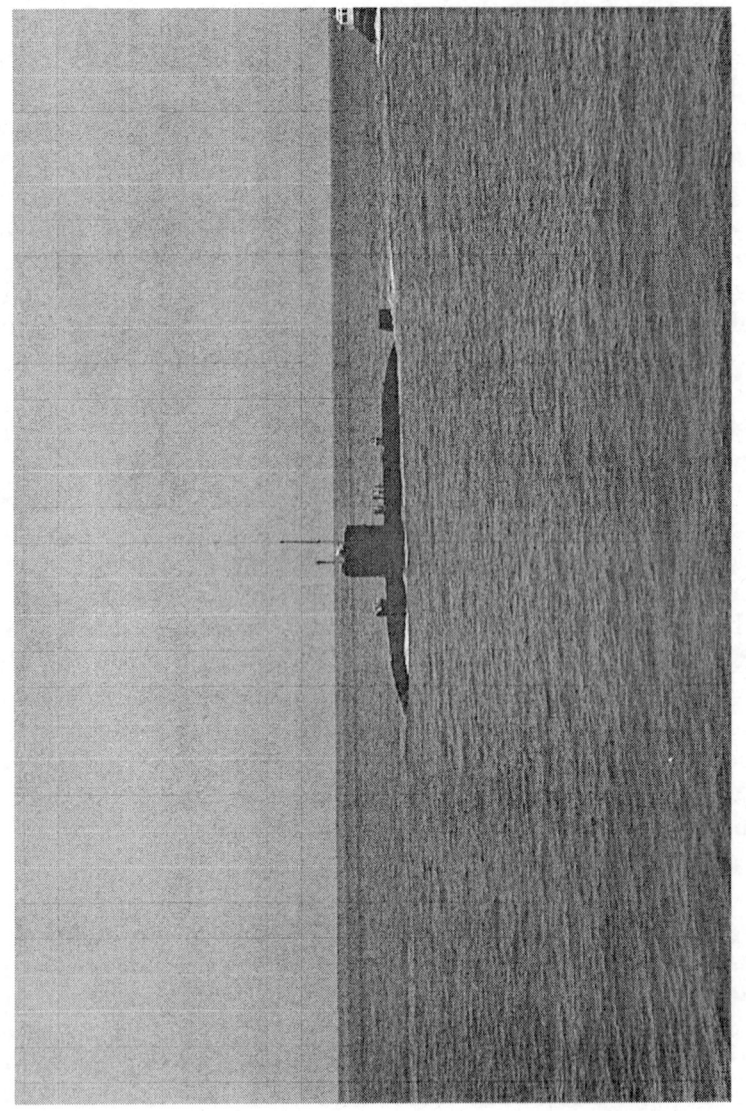

Our fascination with water drives us to explore its depths as far as we are able

maidens who present the gift of magic to those deemed worthy. The creatures which live in Water capture the imagination. Those which we can see such as fishes and Water mammals fascinate many of us. Those we cannot see in the depths of the ocean or lochs give rise to fantastic tales of giant squids, lost aquatic dinosaurs or serpents of diverse sorts. Water expands the imagination like a distorting mirror, one which makes all things look larger and indistinct. It is this very distortion which can lead to new vistas of imagination, or to madness.

Water is central to all magic in its cleansing aspect. Many magical traditions require the magician to bathe before commencing an act of magic, and some require the cleansing of various objects. Spells which involve Water will invariably involve some reference to this aspect of Water, yet there is still more to Water and especially to Water spirits. The symbolism of Water encompasses creativity in an emotional sense. While artistic inspiration is a thing of Air, it is our emotions which are touched by such things as a moving poem, a piece of music or a painting which speaks to us. We react with emotion to an old tale or a work of fiction written by someone else, because it feeds the spirit of imagination in a different way than when we create our own stories, so in reading the work of another we move fluidly from the creative world of Air into the responsive realm of Water. They say of the world of Faery that as long as the stories are still told, the old ways are not forgotten. Water reflects the realm of Spirit, and it is within our emotions that the Water spirits reach reality.

Invoking or evoking Water spirits can be a rather tricky business, as they are difficult to grasp or to contain in any manner. In general, one can only give direction to a Water spell or spirit, knowing that the eventual outcome will ultimately be unpredictable in its detail.

Water is an element which can be easily experienced first hand. While a spell performed at the seaside or at the edge of a pond, river or stream may be very effective, one may choose to fully experience the element by direct immersion. This may be uncomfortable in cold Water which could be distracting, but is very satisfying in warmer conditions where the feeling of ultimate enfoldment in the warm Waters of life is likely to add a sense of empowerment to whatever magic one chooses to perform within this sphere of natural magic. Water spells may even be performed in the bath.

Seeking Water spirits in nature however, usually involves going outside. Indoor Water supplies will naturally contain some form of Water spirit, but these are transient spirits which lack the aged solidity of Water sources which are found in nature. Even human made ponds are likely to have been established for some time, and the proximity of newly made wells and ponds to the rest of nature very quickly attracts the attention of elementals in the location. A newly established Water spirit which inhabits such a place will spontaneously merge with local spirits of dew and other natural moisture to form a spirit which is both old and new, and the newness will soon fade as the Water itself gives life to microorganisms, algae and small plants. Water is the giver of life, which again associates it with the feminine principle of creation.

This does not render the position of Water spirits in the home as unimportant, far from it. What the spirit in a freshly poured glass of Water lacks in the sense of timelessness, it gains in the vitality of freshness. Despite the unnatural processes which humans subject their Water supplies to in order to clean out impurities, the Water itself maintains the life-giving spirit which is its essential self. It may lack some of the natural minerals which we must replace elsewhere, but it is still fresh Water. It is essential to life.

Water must move and change to maintain this life-giving property. Water which does not move or produce some form of life stagnates, and becomes poison. One may ask, why does this not happen in still ponds or wells where Water seems to stay constant rather than moving as in a river or ocean. This is because the Water in such a source creates its own ecosystem, and this cycle of life maintains the life giving properties of the Water itself.

Water must move and change to live, as do we who are so much consistent of Water. Humans are driven by emotions as much as by physical needs. Even the most seemingly emotionless scientist is driven by a passion for discovery. We are driven by nature to grow, to learn and to discover. Those who lose their zest for life very quickly shrivel into nothingness. It is that which we sometimes call the 'human spirit', the need to do something more than merely to exist, which can lead a downtrodden person back to the world of the living, or another person into the realms of art and science where there is much to discover or to create.

The importance of emotion to our species has led to some very deep and dark recesses of imagination when it comes to Water spirits in folklore. Besides the mysterious creatures of the deep mentioned earlier, many tales tell of underwater kingdoms of fairy or other creatures, often including beautiful maidens who bring magical gifts to mortals on the land. Perhaps the most famous of these is the Lady of the Lake from the Arthurian legends, who provides the sword Excaliber to Arthur to aid his quest to unify the peoples of England, then receives it back in her keeping upon his death, to keep it safe until his return in a reincarnated form. Water spirits in folklore are often changeable and moody, as will be seen in a later chapter.

Water conceals many hazards, yet is infinitely inviting and comfortable to swim in if appropriate safety precautions are observed. The bouyancy of Water magically frees us of the limitations of gravity, and therein lies an important lesson in dealing with Water magic. Water can seep through some very stringent limitations. This can be good in that a spell involving a Water spirit may slip through some very difficult conditions. On the other hand, one must remember that the Water spell may just as easily spread beyond the boundaries that have been set for it. In most cases, this need not be a major problem depending on the nature of the spell. However, the magician who works with Water should always be aware that there is likely to be some 'bleed-through', and should anticipate the possibility of having to contend with some 'mopping up'.

The spirit of a body of Water usually has an easily perceived presence. Water is well known to have a powerful effect on human emotions by doing nothing more than being present. As a Water sign myself, I find it necessary to live near Water. Most of my life has been spent within a reasonable distance of an ocean. At present, my home is just a few yards from a major river crossing. On the very few occasions that I have spent a little time living away from Water, I was never able to feel 'at home' in the place. Even people who do not react to Water quite this strongly will find peace at the side of a still pool or encouragement from a trip to the seaside, except possibly for those who come to the Waters edge in despair. Those who are drowning in emotion may well seek drowning in the very element which could help them to find a less tragic sense of peace. Water inspires the depths of emotion, but those depths can turn to the sweet or the sour.

Those who visit a particular place of Water on a regular basis will form a natural bond with the attendant Water spirit. Many people both famous and obscure have found serenity at the side of a pond near their home, or at the site of a holy well. Holy wells in particular are known for recurrent magic, particularly healing or wish fulfilment. Those who live near such a well are likely to find themselves drawn to the well on occasion, just as others will visit their pond or the nearby seaside. The Water, symbolic of the deep unconscious, entices the consciousness and demands the release of stresses and troubles. It lures the natural intuitive mind, allowing solutions to become clear or psychic abilities to surface. Water runs deep within us both physically and spiritually, although sometimes it will demand its sacrifice. This too is illustrated in folklore.

Water, in and of itself, is not destructive. It is only when it is whipped up by Air, thrown about by the Earth, boiled by Fire or unnaturally contained and then released by humans that the very weight of its fluid mass becomes a danger to those who happen to be in the way. Water conceals both dangerous creatures such as sharks, and delightful, helpful creatures such as dolphins, who have been known to rescue shipwrecked sailors and take them to land. Those who drown generally do so because of hyperthermia, because they have been caught in underwater plants or have got themselves into a situation where they have lost the strength to swim. Sailors of days gone by who prayed to Neptune or Poseidon to give them safe journey over the sea might have been well advised to consult Air and Earth deities as well. Without the interference of winds or undersea earthquakes, the sea would be ever calm, moving only in relation to the gravitational pull of the Moon. The spirit of Water is essentially calm, and it will always return to a calm state once is ceases to be disturbed by external phenomena.

Water correspondences lean toward the intuitive, and may sometimes be abstract. In understanding the nature of Water spirits we come to learn new forms of perception and insight, and can rediscover the realm of instinct and precognition which still exist in the other creatures of nature, both on land and in Water. The intuitive principle is more essential to our survival than we often realize. It is even more vital in the realm of magic, where so much depends on the 'knowing'. It is this principle which we seek to embrace as we discover the nature of the spirits of the Water.

2

Types of Water Spirits

Water holds much of the symbolism which is of central importance to fairy lore. It has a dual nature; that which creates life and provides nourishment, and that which takes lives. Naturally, the divinities which are associated with Water reflect this dual nature. Like the rivers, pools and other bodies of Water which they inhabit, the Water elementals are known for the dual qualities of abundance and treachery.

The names and forms which these Water creatures take are far too numerous to list completely in a single chapter, but there are some basic 'types' which seem to repeat in different cultures by many names. Alastair MacGregor in his book on scots folklore, The Peat-Fire Flame, gives several accounts of one of these basic types, the seal women. These Water spirits typically discard their fishtail garments and come ashore to marry a human, beget children and eventually are drawn back to the sea. They abandon the human husband and their children to return to their Watery world, never to be seen again.

The feminine aspect of Water spirits arises in several general themes of Water fairy lore. Water spirits who appear as beautiful women are among the best known legends. These include the classical Mermaid or Loreleii, which are closely related to the legend of the Morgan. The Morgan in legend is an eternally young sea fairy whose passion leads her to seduce mortals, although her need for human love is never

satisfied. This drives her to despair, and she rises to the surface at night to brush her fine hair and sing her plaintive song, which often draws sailors toward her. They are subsequently shipwrecked on the rocks, and the Morgan 'takes' one to be her husband.

Water maidens recur again as spirits of magical wells or of lakes and pools who sometimes bear gifts or grant wishes. The most famous of these is undoubtedly the Lady of the Lake of Arthurian legend, who rises from her lake to present the magical sword Excaliber to the once and future King of legend. Other female lake spirits cross into the realm of animism and take the form of water-fowl, particularly swans.

Certain animals are associated with Water spirits, most notably the Salmon of Wisdom which swims in the Pool of Inspiration and Foreknowledge. The symbolism of this knowledgeable fish spills over into some of the Celtic fairy folk tales, where the little people are reported to wear salmon-skin caps. Celtic peoples are known to have had a staunch reverence for Water spirits. Many treasures have been found in lakes, which are considered to provide inviolable protection. Offerings, including coins, jewellery and valuable weapons, were frequently made to the spirits of Watery places.

Water spirits may appear to the human observer in a variety of odd guises. Some tales of Water creatures both friendly and hazardous may be partially the result of hallucination in difficult circumstances as psychologists would have us believe, but the forms these creatures take have maintained a certain amount of consistency over hundreds of years which defies the logical arguments that they are no more than forms created by the imagination after having heard the tales. I personally have no doubt that some Water spirits can and will intentionally take on a form above or near Water which can be perceived by humans in order to elicit a reaction. More commonly, Water spirits will take their form within the Water, needing no actual form to observe their human subject, yet sometimes allowing themselves to be observed for a fleeting moment. It is easy in such a situation to dismiss a face, a curious fish, or any number of other manifestations as no more than a trick of reflected light or passing Water creatures of the more mundane sort. Some scientists insist that sightings of mermaids in the sea are the result of imagination and a passing manatee. This explanation in particular is laughable to anyone who has actually seen a manatee. Mermaid sightings over the centuries have been far too numerous for such an explanation to hold any credence.

Water spirits which are reputed to appear on land include animals which appear in the vicinity of Water. These include toad elementals, Water horses and bulls and oddly, Black Dogs. Sightings of Black dogs are still reported in or near certain rivers, just as 'white lady' ghosts recur in the vicinity of wells.

In general, Water spirits or attendant animals who dwell in or near rivers and streams tend to be less dangerous than their counterparts who live in the seas and lakes, although one who has been nearly drowned by a Kelpie is unlikely to dwell on the comparison with a Leviathan or a sea nymph. Certain trees are also associated with Water spirit activity, especially Alder, one of the catkin-bearing trees. Alder is resistant to wet rot, and ancient lake dwellers were dependent upon it. In fairy lore, some Water spirits and mysterious white horses issue from magical gateways hidden among clumps of Alder.

Faerie islands are closely associated with Water spirits. The Irish in particular have many faerie islands inherent in their folklore. These islands are often the homes of fairies, gods or even the dead in the later Christian associations of fairies as the spirits of the dead which will be more fully explained in Spirits of the Aether.

Faerie islands are generally thought to be utopias of happiness, peace and plenty, where it is always Spring and there is no aging, disease or work. Some of them are inhabited by weird and monstrous beasts. Some faerie islands float while others are submerged, rising above the surface only at night or periodically such as every seven years. They can never be found when looked for, but only happened upon at times of need or when one's presence is desired by one of the previously described Water maidens.

Following is a small sampling of some of the better known Water spirits of legend and folklore;

BEAN-NIGHE (Gaelic)
A type of banshee who haunts the rivers and streams of Scotland and Ireland, washing the blood-stained garments of those who are about to die. They are reputed to be the ghosts of women who died in childbirth and are fated to perform their task until the time when they would normally have died.

SHELLYCOAT (Scottish)
So named because he wears shells on his coat which clatter when he moves. He takes pleasure in leading travellers astray, a frequent theme among Water spirits.

ALVEN (Dutch)
An insubstantial spirit which glides over water in rivers and streams, and can also glide through currents. It is a very powerful spirit which controls many bodies of water, particularly the River Elbe. Alven are shape changers, another common theme of Water spirits.

NIXEN AND WATER MEN (German and Norse)
Fresh Water spirits which guard the way to elfland. They seduce young girls and take them to their underwater homes (a counterpart of the Water maiden theme). The Nix appear on the surface of water, singing and harp playing, raise storms, warn of drownings, and teach humans the art of fiddling if they are given gifts of white or black goats. The unwary human may find that he wont be able to stop fiddling on such a gift until someone cuts the strings.

ASRAI (British)
Full Moon night is called Asrai night, when these spirits come to the surface of water to look at the Moon once every century. A single ray of sunlight will melt them into a pool of water. They are benevolent and shy, live deep underwater in lake bottoms or in the sea, and appear as small, beautiful women with long green hair.

LEVIATHAN (Hebrew)
Originally depicted in the Christian Bible as a crocodile or the great python of Egyptian monuments, in common usage as any large, scaly sea monster. Sometimes referred to as the Water aspect of the Christian devil.

GWAGGED ANNWN (Welsh)
Lake maidens; tall, blond and immortal. They live in rich palaces under lakes and come to land to dance, hunt or stroll near the lake. There may be an association with the Arthurian Lady of the Lake.

NEREIDES (Mediterranean)
In some tales, these travel in whirlwinds through Air but live in rivers, springs, wells, as well as some mountain locations

and caves. In Greek mythology they are the daughters of the sea god Nereus, who attended Neptune. They ride on seahorses.

LADY OF THE LAKE (British)
Romantisized through the Arthurian legends, the Lady of the Lake is claimed by some sources to be originally Le Fata Morgana, a Water fairy who raised storms at sea. This creates speculation as to the polarity of the Lady of the Lake with Morgan LeFay in the legends.

SELKIES (Scottish)
Selkies live in the seas around Orkney and Shetland and resemble seals. A female is able to shed her seal skin and come ashore as a beautiful maiden. If a mortal man finds this skin, she can be forced to become his wife, but if she should ever find the skin she immediately returns to the sea. Male selkies raise storms and overturn boats to avenge seal slaughter.

MERMAID (Multi-cultural)
Half human woman, half fish. In some versions they entice humans with their song and cause ship-wrecking storms. In others, they rescue drowning sailors and bring them safely to land. Still more legends claim that they desire human legs and husbands, and in many tales a way is found to obtain this goal, often at a terrible price. Sometimes inhabits streams, pools or lakes, as well as the sea.

MERROW (Irish)
Merpeople who wear red-feathered caps which help propel them to their watery homes. The females are beautiful and sometimes marry human men because the males are very

ugly, but good-natured. Both sometimes come ashore as little hornless cattle.

CABYLL-USHTEY (Isle of Man)
A Water horse known to steal cattle or maidens.

WATER LEAPER (Welsh)
A Water spirit which preys on Welsh fishermen.

URISK (Scotland)
A solitary fairy who haunts lonely pools. He will seek out human company, but his appearance terrifies those he approaches.

GLASTIG (Scottish)
This Water fairy is part seductive woman, part goat. The goat attributes are hidden under her green dress. She lures men to dance with her before feeding vampire-like on their blood, but can also tend children or old people or herd cattle for farmers.

KELPIE (Scotland)
The Kelpie if often seen in the form of a horse. It haunts rivers and streams and allows unsuspecting travellers to mount him, then dashes into the Water and dunks or drowns him. The term is associated with the Each-Uisge which is a malevolent Water-horse. The Highland Water horse haunts the sea and sea lochs, changes shape often, and takes victims into water and devours them leaving their liver to float home. Similar is the Tarbh-Uisge, a Water-bull which is sometimes malevolent, but sometimes benevolent.

The terms 'Kelpie' or 'Each-Uisge' are sometimes used to describe what is known in Northern England as a 'Water Dobbie'. One of the most common beliefs regarding dobbies is that one may be protected from them by keeping a dobbie-stone in the house. This is a piece of limestone which has a hole worn by Water through the middle. It is said to "ward off witches and evil spirits, especially dobbies", and some believe that Gypsies will not call on homes where such a stone is hung by the door. One area where tales and superstitions associated with Water horses or dobbies are widespread is the Sedbergh area, which Guy Ragland Phillips writes about in his book, Brigantia. Here we find the Black Horse of Bush Howe, which is a dark outline of a large black horse which dominates the valley of Long Rigg Beck. It is said that 'once you have seen it, then you will never pass by without looking'. Some deny its existence, but this horse was observed first hand by Ragland Phillips, although he was unable to photograph it. Clouds often fall on this valley, and the mists prevented photography on his first visit. Camera misfunction was to blame for his inability to photograph the horse on a second visit, then on a third visit the horse was clearly visible in bright sunshine, yet the photographs which resulted were very misty. Further expeditions also resulted in negative results. By contrast, artist Jeremy Scott, inspired by the accounts of Ragland Phillips, found the horse much more cooperative as he relates;

"Several years ago, after spending a cold Winter's night at Long Meg for the Winter Solstice, I found myself in the Sedbergh area. I had it in mind to look for the Black Horse as I approached the Howgills from the Kendal side. At the same moment that I could see the Howgills, my eye fell on it. I immediately stopped the car to take my first photo. Usually the Howgills are covered in mist or low cloud as are most of the fells of that area, but that day was gorgeous and clear, rather like a frozen Winterland. I felt that I was on to a good thing.

The Black Horse of Bush Howe. Photo by Jeremy Scott

A nearby pond known for water lilies

"I drove through Sedbergh and out on the Howgill road. This is a very tight road with only one lane in places and high walls on each side. That day it was covered with black ice. Trying to keep the car on the road, as well as avoiding hitting anything coming the other way while also looking for the Black Horse was quite vexing. At last I reached a spot near the path where I could park the car. I set off on foot up this path with Long Rigg Beck to my left. I soon realized that I was on the wrong path and even though the Black Horse looked quite close and inviting, it was late afternoon so I decided to let common sense prevail for once and left it until the next day.

"Next morning was cold and clear, just like the previous day. I drove up to Howgill, leaving the car in the same place as I had done the day before. I walked up the right track this time, with Long Rigg Beck to my right. The Horse vanished out of sight for a while until I rounded a hill, then appeared again until I crossed Long Rigg Beck. I decided to walk up onto the calf (one of the Howgill fells) as it was quite a steep climb. I branched off the path and walked along the edge of Bush Howe, then it seemed to suddenly appear, just as it had for Guy Ragland Phillips.

"It was a moving feeling, looking upon this legendary horse in the freezing Winter Wonderland. I decided against going up to it as I respected it for letting me get so close and the slope it is on is very steep. I continued up the calf and discovered the most amazing view at the top, which looks out over Morcombe Bay to the West, and over the top of the Howgills to Mallerstang Common and Garsdale Head into Wensleydale to the East.

"Six months later, for Summer Solstice, I returned by the same route to visit the Black Horse in Summer. Its appearance is totally different than it is in Winter. While crossing Long Rigg Beck this time, I stumbled and fell into rather a deep part of it. I couldn't help but imagine that any resident Water dobbie which happened to be around would have been gratified at my misfortune. Dripping wet, I continued. I dried out fairly quickly though, and eventually reached the same vantage point as before. This time I left my bag and proceeded onto the Horse itself. The Horse is made up of rocks and may be just a natural scree, but it does have a very defined shape with an eye. I performed a little ritual and left some lentils and apples as an offering. I snapped some more photos, and spent the rest of the afternoon sunbathing and listening to 'Pink Floyd' tapes.

"My camera was just a 'cheap and nasty' 110 which had had beer and suncream spilt on it and has fallen into the sea and off of moterbikes, so I was pleasantly surprised to see that rather than the fuzzy photos which I had been expecting from reading the exploits of Guy Ragland Phillips, every frame came out clear and were some of the best prints I had had from that camera.

"I still do not know whether the Horse is man-made or just a natural scree and am not really concerned either way, but it is interesting to note that there is an ancient ford and the remains of three possible bronze/stone age round huts where Long Rigg Beck joins another stream which comes down off the calf. It is known that there are wild ponies living on the Howgills which may well be descendants of those which were used by the Brigantes. I haven't seen them myself as they are as illusive as the Black Horse itself.

"I believe that it is true that once you have seen the Black Horse, you always look out for it. I cannot drive up the M6 past Howgill without looking for it. This isn't a very clever thing to do when the moterway is busy, but it can also be seen from the train as it enters the Lune Gorge. Once you know it is there, it brings a bit of magic into the area."

The examples of Water spirits listed in this chapter are a very small sampling of a vast panorama of tales of Water spirits in folklore, although they are representative of several of the most common themes. The interested reader is encouraged to read the folklore books which are included in the bibliography of this volume, as well as other books on fairy folklore which may not have been included.

The Water spirits which inhabit the natural world are, in some cases, not so far removed from the fanciful creatures of folklore. Water and its hidden depths hides more than archetypes, it also conceals much of what lies undiscovered by the scientific community, which includes unknown creatures which continue to be sighted and in some cases, eventually proven to exist in very solid form.

The spirits of Water may sometimes imitate these forms, teasing the human observer and maintaining the mystery which lies behind the unseen. There is much evidence that Water spirits which attend specific bodies of Water are able to travel over land near the source of Water, hence the stories of well guardians and animal or ghostly custodians of pools, lakes and rivers. Artistic representations of Water spirits will often adopt one of these legendary forms, the most common perhaps being depictions of little fairies who skim the surface of a pool or spring on the leaves of Water lilies accompanied by their toad familiars and the occasional fish with wise countenance. Films tend to depict the more ferocious aspects of Water spirits in the form of giant squids or sea monsters, occasionally allowing a benevolent sea creature to grace the celluloid as in the film Loch Ness, where the legendary dinosaur creatures of the loch befriend a little Scottish girl who refers to them as 'the Kelpies', rather acutely ignoring the traditionally malevolent associations of Water Kelpies.

Many Water spirits seem to be very much 'place' spirits. While Water, as an element, is similar to Air and Fire in that the actual substance (and therefore the minute spirits) of the element is ever changing, creating a larger mass from infinite minute components, the overall body of Water maintains an attendant spirit which is little effected by the constantly changing quantities of actual fluid by evaporation or source Water. Quite often, trying to determine the feeding source of a body of Water can be difficult or impossible, and is frequently left to assumption. Water spirits are often perceived as 'place' guardians.

These guardians vary in temperament, but their reputations may sometimes suffer from human acumen. The guardian spirit of an ocean is a formidable concept, and is represented by magnificent gods such as the Roman Neptune or Greek Poseidon. The guardian spirit of a lake or river where people have drowned may be assessed as malevolent, pulling victims under the surface by way of sacrifice, yet the actual Water spirit may be blameless of human misfortune...or not. One should never be too dismissive of possible origins of folktales, particularly if drownings reoccur too often in the same locality. It could be the perfectly logical result of an underwater hazard, but then again one must remember that the fishes must eat to continue the biological ecosystem which keeps a contained source of Water 'alive'. Who is to say whether a Water spirit may in some instances serve as predator? Aboriginal cultures will often refer to a source of stagnant Water as being possessed by evil spirits, yet this is what happens when the ecosystem in the Water dies.

Whether a particular Water spirit is regarded as benevolent or malevolent is rather dependent on the experiences of those who encounter the source of Water. In the end, Water spirits are like magic; neither good nor evil in substance. In many of their forms, they are no more or less than the spirit guardians of a specific source of Water. This is most clearly illustrated in the legends of spirits of sacred wells.

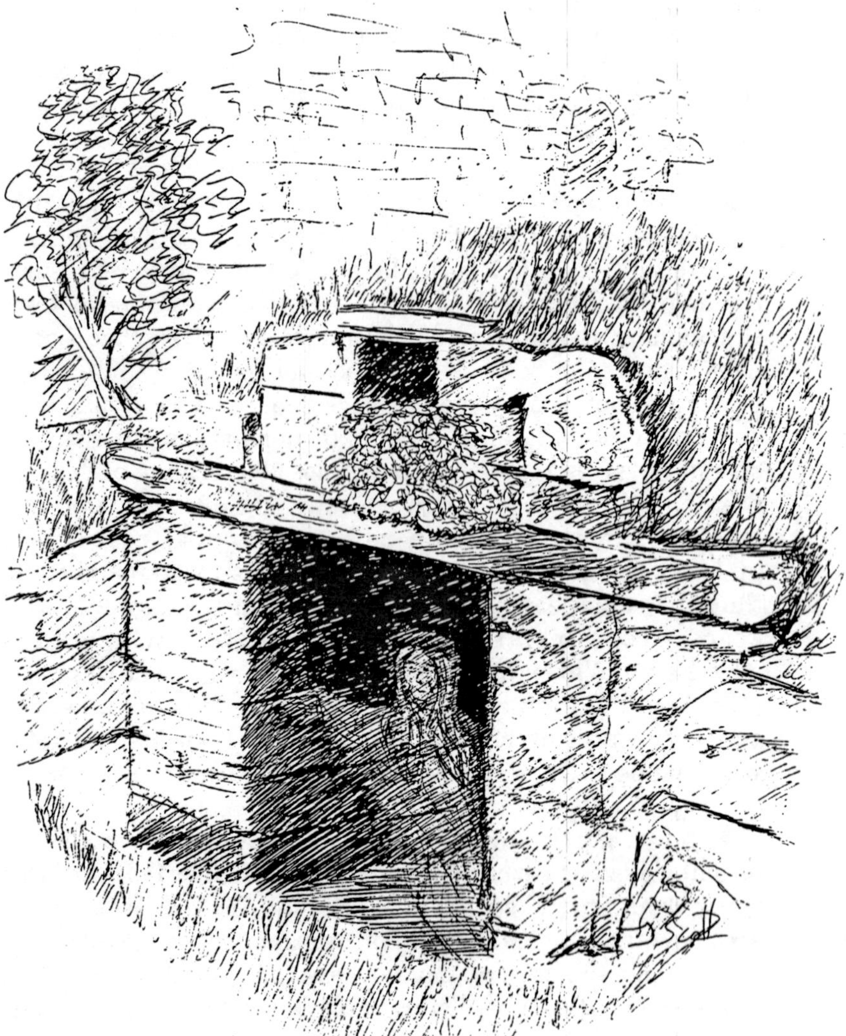

3

In the Depths of a Well

The very thought of a sacred well brings forth images of magic, of spirits and of the depths of mystery from whence all needs are fulfilled. The romanticism which exudes from the very notion of deep and Watery places of worship reaches into a part of the soul which transcends religion, yet also entices one into a level of emotional melding with the essence of Spirit which craves singularity, a personal identification with the divine which says; "This is my path, and that of my people. It is sacred to us."

Mythology and Origins of Sacred Wells

The beginnings or creation of wells are often cloaked in legends. One common theme for lake worship begins as a sacred well which overflows after someone leaves the lid off. It then becomes a lake with a female guardian spirit. Well spirits are most often female, but it is common knowledge that many female Water divinities are later renamed for male saints.

Wells are considered to be a reflection of, or door to, the 'otherworld' in popular folklore, and some wells such as Sancreed in West Penwith (Cornwall) still carry these specific associations. Many tales of coaches vanishing into pools and wells refer to the Celtic belief in places of Water as a gateway to the otherworld, the land of Faery. Other stories of treasure which is to be found at the bottom of a well or other source of contained Water are symbolic of the sanctity of Water itself.

There are well associations with Arthur and Merlin, as well as the legendary Lady of the Lake. There are several contenders for identification as the pool where Excaliber was thrown at the end of Arthur's life, mostly with close associations with Glastonbury.

A romance known as *The Conte del Graal* recounts the manner in which the land of Logres (present English Midlands) was laid waste by an impious act of King Amangons. The tale says that he did wrong to a damsel of the well who fed wayfarers and then he carried off her golden cup, thus adding injury to insult so that "never more came damsels out of springs to comfort the wanderer." It is said that thereafter the grass withered and the land became waste.

The land of Logres has associations with labyrinths, which have a Water connection and play a part of the mythology regarding the gate to the 'otherworld'. Avalon is known to have once been surrounded by Water, and the common belief is that the Tor in modern day Glastonbury is the site of ancient Avalon. The Tor is characterized by an elaborate labyrinth design which is carved into the Earth itself.

Many wells are associated with ghostly 'white ladies' or well fairies. Some are named for fairies such as Fairie's Well near Hardhorn (Lancaster), Fairy Well on Irby Heath (Cheshire) and Laugharne (Carmarthen) and Fordoun Hill (Kincardine), and Pixy Well or Pisky Well which is a popular name throughout the West Country, not to mention Mab Well at Egton, North Yorkshire. It is claimed that fairies have been seen at some wells, including Ilkley Wells (West Yorkshire).

Much of history tells us that sacred wells come from Pagan roots, many of which are later taken over by Christians and renamed for saints. For many sacred wells in Britain and Europe this is true, yet it is also true that some wells actually have secular beginnings, as needed sources of Water for settlements which may have later become associated with spirit worship. There are also wells which the Christians may claim as their own, as their religion has a long tradition of Water reverence which is completely separate from Pagan hydrolatry.

The Celts were head-hunters. For them, the head symbolized divine power and the source of the attributes of healing, fertility, wisdom and prophecy. Ancient Celtic well spirits or deities often originate from head cults. There is much evidence for an historic cult of wells throughout Britain, which survives in such customs as drinking from a skull kept at a well. Some of these skulls are decorated with gold. At some wells drinking from the skull was a requirement for the magic to work. An Oak tree by a well may well indicate the site of an early head cult, as the Oak was sacred to this culture.

Many historic wells have been lost in the last 100 years by development. Not all of them have necessarily been holy or sacred wells, as many of these wells have existed as boundary markers and simply as sources of Water near villages. However, Water which is found in response to need has a way of becoming associated with religious munificence. Although it is true that many wells have been renamed for Christian saints to distract the local populace from their Pagan origins, tales are frequently told of wells which appear as the result of one saint or another who plunges his staff into the Earth in time of drought, resulting in the discovery of an underground spring which becomes a holy well. Some would argue that these tales are yet another 'cover' for Christian absorption of a Pagan well which is discovered through dowsing, but it is not always possible for archaeologists to determine definite origins for a specific well and in some cases a Christian origin actually seems more likely than a Pagan one.

This does not detract from the obvious Pagan origins of the majority of wells found in Britain, many of which are identified by obvious references in their names such as 'Lady Well' or 'Fairy Well', as mentioned earlier. These names appear frequently in various locations. A comprehensive list of examples of specific wells with these associations may be found in the book, *The Living Stream* by James Rattue, and many more examples can be found in *Holy Places of Celtic Britain* by Mick Sharp, both of which are listed in the Bibliography and are highly recommended to the student of well lore.

The various religious associations with sacred or holy wells can present a varied and complicated history to the serious inquirer. The mixtures of early head cults and later Pagan customs are often combined with Christian attitudes toward holy wells which change depending on historic period as well as location. The Roman Emperors Constantine, Valentinian and Theodosius forbid worship of stones, trees and fountains in an attempt to put an end to these forms of Pagan worship, yet at a time when well worship was seriously discouraged in Rome, small Christian cults in Britain were absorbing the use of local wells or using wells of their own for baptisms.

Chapels and abbeys were built to enclose some popular wells, which besides providing Water for baptisms and other purposes, also attracted the attendance of the local populace. Some examples of enclosed wells may be found at Dumfermline Abbey in Fife, Beverley Minster in Humberside, St. Patrick's at Aspatria and St. Oswald's at Kirkoswald. Historic wells of uncertain origin have been found at St. Patrick's Cathedral in Dublin, Winchester Cathedral, Wells Cathedral, Exeter Cathedral and in the crypt and foundations of York Minster as well as the crypt of Glasgow Cathedral. Wells frequently appear in or near minsters. In York Minster for example, there are two actual wells as well as at least two fonts.

The early medieval church was happy to create its own holy wells. They developed their own form of well cults and in some cases were willing to adopt some elements of Pagan practices regarding these wells. The Bishop Cuthbert in the tenth century created a holy well on Inner Farne, yet the church was largely hostile to wells during that century. Christians use Water in ritual for the sacrament that admits people into the church, for baptism and as Holy Water for blessings. Sacred vessels must be washed. Water is purifier and transmitter of spiritual power. It is no surprise then that Christians widely adopt holy wells of other cultures. Some examples of these wells are more prominent than others, such as Thor's Well at Thorsas, Norway which is now known as St. Thor's. Possibly the best known healing well in Britain is Chalice Well at Glastonbury, which has both Christian and Pagan associations. It has a wrought-iron cover which was donated by Frederick Bligh Bond after the First World War as a peace offering. It is decorated with two circles which represent the interlocking worlds of spirit and substance. The healing Waters of this well are so well known that even Prince Charles has been seen in worldwide news to allow them to flow over an injured arm in hopes of obtaining a speedy recovery.

Wishing wells came into being when religious attitudes were changing and wells were being renamed. Rather than offer a prayer to the saint, the local people would make a wish. For the purposes of this book, the actual origin for any given well is less important than the nature of the Water spirit which inhabits it. This we will come back to after examining some of the customs and traditions associated with sacred wells.

Well Customs and Traditions
The traditions associated with various wells often hold a combination of Pagan and Christian origins. Each well seems to have its own unique customs, yet there are repeating

themes which reflect on the history of the specific wells. Some wells like St. Maughold's Well on the Isle of Man require an act of drinking the Water and sitting in a 'Saint's Chair' nearby, which will be in the form of a natural or carved rock structure, in order to obtain some benefit such as a healing of disease or sometimes infertility, which is an indication of earlier Pagan superstition which would predate the addition of the saint's chair. In the case of St. Maughold's Well, the performance of the appropriate observances is known for the cure of sore eyes and infertility. Many wells are associated with specific types of healing. Among them are; the Well of Youth at Dun Iona which requires those seeking healing or youth of spirit to wash in its Waters at dawn; Madron Well in Cornwall which is associated with curing skin diseases and divination; St. Fillian's Pool at Tyndrum, Scotland, St. Gwenfaen's Well at Rhoscolyn, Anglesey, and St. Non's Well at Altarnun, Cornwall which are known for curing mental illness.

The Pagan legacies in well tradition become apparent through certain aspects of local customs. Traditional offerings at wells such as coins, pins, and butter are typical of wells with fairy associations or those which are associated with fertility, such as St. Augustine's Well at Cerne Abbas, Dorset. Many wells, including some which have been claimed by Christian practice, still attract visitors at holidays such as Lammas - 12 August (old pagan Lugnassah); Beltane - 1 May or old Celtic Beltane - 12 May; Samhain - 1 November; Imbolc - 1 February; and Midsummer - 21 June as well as various saint's days.

Fairies are believed to inhabit certain wells, most notably Minchmoor Well or Cheese Well in Peeblesshire. Often these wells are considered to be in charge of a fairy to whom an offering must be made--a pin, a coin or a piece of cheese. The wells in Brayton, Harphan, Holderness, and Atwick, in Yorkshire, and Wooler, in Northumberland as well as

Inverness are presided over by fairies or spirits. It is believed that women who suspected their babies of being changlings left them there over night and in the morning found their own infants. Robin Round Cap Well in East Yorkshire is reported to be haunted by a brownie. The list goes on. In France, hundreds of wells are under the tutelage of "saints" who are actually fairies disguised by Christian piety.

Healings are often reported to have been effected at wells, and in one case at Madron Well in Cornwall in 1640 the cure was witnessed by a bishop. These healings generally consisted of drinking the Water and performing other rituals such as walking around the well three times or drinking specifically from a special cup or skull.

Water which had washed or been drunk from holy relics was believed to have healing powers, or the Water from the well itself was used for washing the affliction. Dipping heads, stones, or other objects was believed to give them magical abilities. Charm stones, dipped in holy wells, are still used for healing. It is accepted by historians that the traditional dances round the wells of England must come from an ancient Pagan past, and were probably part of a ritual associated with the well.

Stone megaliths are often found near wells, and there is a belief that these have served as 'guardians' for the wells. Some wells are known for spiritual rather than healing powers, and their symbolism falls well into the realms of magic. Alder, Oak or Hazel trees are commonly found near wells and other sources of sacred Waters, and like the megaliths, are sometimes believed to be 'guardians' of the Water source. Stone circles are also found near wells including at Drumlanrig and Tullybelton. Those which have single megalithic guardians are often in conjunction with trees, particularly Alder and Oak.

Well in the crypt of York Minster

Italian well presided over by Bacchus

Castaway well at East witton, also known as Diana's Well or Slaverton Sol

Interior of Robin Hood's Well at West Witton, now nearly lost to erosion

The Dripping Well at Knaresborough

The author at Chalice Well, Glastonbury

Jeremy Scott at Lime Trees Well, decorated with his own sculpture

A classic wishing well

The trees which are found near these wells are likely to be decorated with offerings. Some have old coins hammered into the bark, but in these ecological days it is more likely to find evidence of another old custom, strips of cloth hung on branches. These should be of natural fibre, as the tradition originates with the belief that the cloth which bound a wound left on a tree would cause the wound to heal as the cloth moulders and disintegrates. This could take a very long time with modern synthetic fabrics. Brightly coloured strips of cotton have become a modern day offering for the trees which watch over the sacred wells. These can still be found at many wells, among them are Virtuous Well at Trellech, Gwent where the strips of cloth hang from nearby Hazel trees and Madron Well at Penzance. They are also found at St. Gundred's Well (or St. Conan's Well) at Roche, Cornwall, which is also known specifically for healing ailments of children's eyes. Another well, known specifically for healing children, is St. Non's Well at St. David's, Dyfed where children were dipped and offerings of such things as pins and pebbles were made. Ritually damaged coins were given as offerings at the hot spring at Bath near the baths complex (Roman name Aquae Sulis, named after the goddess Sulis, linked with Minerva and was then known as Sulis Minerva) in exchange for healings or curses which were submitted on clay tablets.

Healing wells will generally receive offerings of pins or coins, and this sometimes includes rituals such as circumnavigating the well sunwise a specific number of times. The sunwise (deosil) direction is important, although there is one exception in Caithness where it is customary to reverse this direction. Moving deosil reflects the movement of the Sun, which is a way of keeping in harmony with cosmic forces. It is reflected in many folk customs, such as stirring a pot 'with the Sun'.

Wells are known for augurs. This may take the form of a well spirit who simply speaks to the petitioner, or may come in the form of fish or worms whose behaviour determines the predictions. In some cases, a priest reads the animal's movements.

Odd Properties of Sacred Wells

There are tales of wells which move locations when insulted. Wells become insulted when defiled and will stop whatever power they have previously displayed. Insulting behaviour may include washing clothes in a well meant for drinking, throwing dead animals in, immersing animals in healing wells intended for humans, not following prescribed ritual, defiling trees or losing them naturally.

Some wells acquire fame because of odd properties such as never freezing or never drying up. St. Andrew's Well at Kirkandrews-on-Eden (Cumbria) is reputed to be 'not affected by the most intense frost or the longest drought'. Odd noises occur at some wells, including whistling sounds and drumming without the benefit of human drummers which has been observed at Oundle (Northampton), Harphan (Humberside), and Hill Wooton (Warwick). Petrifying wells such as the Dropping Well at Knaresborough (North Yorkshire) which contain large quantities of mineral deposits are known for 'turning objects into stone'. A few rare wells have been reported to produce substances which appear to be milk or blood.

Very rural wells are sometimes attended by women, sometimes reputed to be witches, acting as keepers of wells. Some believe that the magic only works with her assistance, although this often consists only of providing drinking vessels. Many of these may have only been local residents who have taken it upon themselves to maintain the wells.

The healing properties of wells are something which science has tried to explain. One theory is that iron or sulphur rich waters effect cures and that it is not just psychological. In cases where these minerals do not occur in the samples of Water taken from the wells and tested, it is surmised that there may be other elements which are far more subtle and sometimes indiscernible which could be responsible. It is unlikely that any scientist will concede that it may be simply a matter of elemental spirit magic.

The Spirit of the Well

Much of what we may expect from the attendant spirits of wells is reflected in the folklore attached to them. Their forms vary, but are most often either female spirit forms or those of sacred fishes kept in holy wells. Salmon and trout were sacred fish to the Celts, and there have been a few wells where a resident trout was held in such reverence that it was replaced if it should die. Salmon, of course, were more likely to be seen in rivers and are symbolic of the underworld, of life renewed and of procreation.

However, some of the fish guardians in wells have been reported to speak or to wear gold rings or chains. These fish are believed to have been of Spirit rather than flesh. Whatever the truth of this may be, there is no doubt that every well is attended by its own spirit as is any other elemental location of nature. It makes no difference whether it is a sacred pool or a constructed well, it is the Water itself which generates Spirit. The reverence given to these wells will naturally effect the nature of the Water spirit, as does the calm nature of a contained source of the element. Perhaps this is why so many well spirits assume the forms of ghostly white ladies, which have religious significance both to those who follow some form of goddess worship and to the Christians who revere their own goddess in the form of the Virgin Mary. It is this reverence which differentiates well spirits from other spirits of places which are occupied by Water.

4

Places to Find Water Spirits

Apart from sacred or holy wells, there are other bodies of Water which are obvious places where one would expect to find Water spirits. As we have seen in folklore, lakes, springs, ponds, and the sea itself all have their attendant spirits which would seem to periodically appear to humans in various guises if the tales are to be even partially believed. The tales of seal women who discard their fishtail garment and come ashore to marry a human are one example of this. The white ladies who protect sacred wells are another. Visible or not, these spirits of Watery places are easily sensed, even by those who have no noticeable psychic abilities at all. One cannot help but respond to the emotional lure that Water has on us. It draws us like a magnet, enticing us into the depths of the world of Water and its hidden treasures... or hazards.

As with Earth and Fire, the spirits of Watery places are likely to be perceived as changing size with the relative volume of Water, sea and tidal wave deities being very large leviathans or gods while pool and pond spirits are perceived as small and gentle. Yet it is the lake and river spirits, and sometimes the pond spirits, which often become associated with sacrifice by drowning the occasional swimmer, or drawing the sacrifice into its depths in an apparent suicide. Indeed, there are places of Water which have become associated with suicides, where the local superstitions speak of a Water spirit which claims the occasional sacrifice.

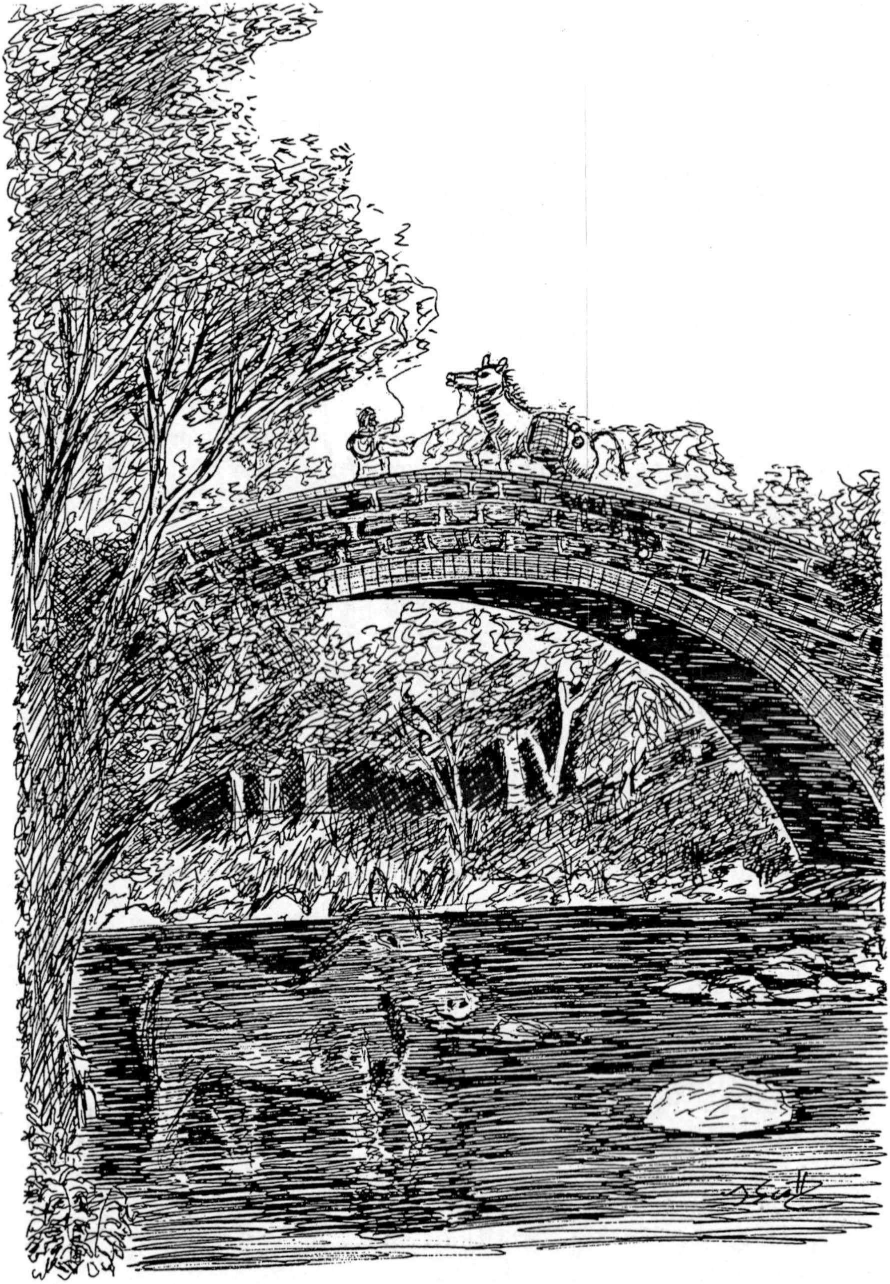

Hierarchy among Water spirits is an odd thing, as Water is ever moving and changing which is not easily understood by the human sense of parameters. Like Fire and Air, the actual element of Water flows from one place to another, while the spirits of both places are able to maintain their individual, if fluctuating, structure. When a river flows over a cliff into a lake, the river has its own guardian spirit as does the lake, and the waterfall which connects the two is also attended by an individual keeper. The individual Water molecules each have their diminutive spirits which make up the gestalt Water spirit of the place, but many of these change their nature as they flow from one to another, much like the individual cells of our own brains which each have their own electrical charge, but make up a communal thought process within their sphere of the brain. The nature of a river spirit is much more active than that of a lake spirit, and the waterfall spirit, whose supply of fluid changes in complete transfusion constantly, actually creates a significant electrical charge by that very movement.

River spirits are rather complex, as there are separate pools within a river which will have a spirit of their own, and yet these are part of the overall river spirit. Spirits connected to certain trees, especially Alder, may also be encompassed by the river spirit if they grow within its path. In folklore, it is said that the Alder tree protects Water spirits.

Spirits of individual places of Water can be cultivated, as is seen in the stories surrounding many human made ponds and wells. Artist Jeremy Scott discovered a guardian 'place' spirit while in the process of clearing a blocked stream which flows into a well made of old horse troughs on a friend's farm. It was seen in his peripheral vision as a man, dressed in sensible brown country clothing. It was also heard walking toward the well, but when the man should have arrived within clear vision, there was simply no one there. There were many speculations as to the nature of this vision, including time slips, but the nature of the vision is very typical of local Water spirits. This one seemed to resemble the owner of the farm, and also seemed to resemble the artist. As the two men do not resemble each other in any way, one can assume that the Water spirit had absorbed much of the essence of the men who had most influenced its source of Water, the farmer by his frequent presence and the artist by his active work on the site which involved a great deal of love and care.

Water is rather unique in that the spirits of Water include those whose abodes are within the Water and are sometimes perceived as some form of swimming creature, yet they also include those spirit guardians who leave the Water and patrol the surrounding area of their especial Watery place. Most Water spirits in art will be depicted as the swimming sort, most often as mermaids or Neptune-like guardians, yet there seems to be an inherent knowledge within us of the more transient nature of Spirit. It is not so difficult to imagine the spirit of a pool of Water rising to the surface for a look about the local landscape or even a short walk in the vicinity. It really isn't much different than imagining the spirit of a flower stepping outside of its petals to attend the well-being of the plant.

There is a natural affinity, almost a melding of Spirit, between a Water spirit and a human who encounters it. This is not surprising considering the amount of Water which comprises our physical being. It is part of the reason that we respond to places of Water on an emotional level, either being drawn into it or reacting with unexplained fear to a particular place, such as the proverbial dark pool. It is almost an automatic response to 'reach out' our emotions to a Water spirit which we encounter.

In the experience related in *Spirits of the Earth* and *Spirits of the Air* when I encountered Air spirits in an otherworld place,

I was very much aware of the spirit of the small stream where I began to sink on my first encounter. It was this awareness which allowed me to remain calm, *knowing* that the stream spirit meant no harm and intended to let me pass all along. It was also this awareness which allowed me to try crossing the same place on a later occasion, sensing that there was to be no repeat of the previous experience.

Until now, I have spoken in this chapter only about places of Water in the natural world, although some are human constructed and become part of nature over time. Some places of Water are reported to be 'gateways' to the otherworld. In fiction and folklore, these are often depicted as underwater places which humans can exist in magically, sometimes conditionally on staying in contact with a mermaid or other Water creature. All places of Water can be considered magical and it is we who respond to them as such. There are of course Water spirits present in any source of the element, including rain puddles, condensation on a window or the mist in the Air. Some tales of magic speak of magical mist, fog or dew. It is a folk custom to wash one's face in the morning dew on the first day of May to achieve fair skin. Not all fog or dew would be perceived as magical by most people, yet they are each in their own way the stuff of magic and Spirit, and certainly contain a Water spirit. Water from the kitchen tap is still Water, regardless of purifying processes. The cook who boils Water for a stew may well petition the spirit of the boiling Water to fortify those who will partake of it, while the extremist might consider this with every glass of Water which is consumed.

Water is with us in every aspect of our lives. The Water spirit of a place is obvious when one is speaking of a lake or other body of Water, but places which are not primarily of Water are also effected by the spirits of Water which touch the place. Water seeps everywhere. Even the wet rot in the walls of a house will affect the overall 'feel' of the place, far beyond the physical dampness which one may experience. Many 'haunted' houses obtain much of their sinister atmosphere from dampness in the walls, as the spirits of what is usually stagnant Water project their dark emotions into the general atmosphere. The tendency of Water spirits to draw the human spirit to them also contributes to this, as the visitor to the house may not be aware that there is dampness within, or may not be aware of the spiritual feeling of Water entities which invade and entice the unwary human into....what? It is that unknown factor which frightens many. The feeling of being enveloped into this Watery essence is not unlike drowning, yet there is no physical danger. Only the warning signals in the mind which alert us of its potential.

On an emotional level, we respond to Water much more strongly than to any other element. One has only to add a bottled Water cooler to an office to bring an atmosphere of clean efficiency into an otherwise average room. Our response to the processed and purified Water, contained and electrically cooled, is more than a psychological association of this sort of Water with a clerical situation. It is the Water in a sacred place like the Glastonbury Well Gardens which gives the place its feeling of spirituality far more than other influences like the resident plant life or the effects of human visitors. Gently running Water alone brings a feeling of calm which defies explanation.

Water is effected by human presence just as are the other elements, yet the cleansing nature of Water tends to wash away most of the vibratory influences of visitors very quickly. The Water spirit of a place maintains its inherent Spirit when other elements are changed by contact with all who touch them. This creates a very old feeling to the spirits of Water and especially to places of Water. Even a fairly recently constructed pond develops this 'old' feeling in a very short time. It is a trait which is unique to the Water element.

In *Spirits of the Earth*, I spoke of the perceived change in the atmosphere of Stonehenge after dark. This change is partly due to the evening mists. It is that old and ancient feeling which is transmitted through Water which washes away the jumble of vibrations which are left by the daily hoards of tourists. If the tourists were to completely stop visiting the place, that nightly cleansing of both Air and Water (the winds contribute as well) would very likely bring back the feel of foreboding power which this place had when it was first discovered. This power still exists within the place, but can be difficult to fully experience amidst the throngs of varied visitors.

Unlike Earth, the spirit of a place of Water is not effected by having some of its quantity taken away. People have sought the Water of sacred wells and pools for centuries, yet these places are not less potent for the samples which are consumed or taken away. Water renews itself, sometimes mysteriously. Even well educated scientists can sometimes be hard pressed to explain the source of Water in some dewponds, as well as in a few sacred church fonts.

The spirit of a place of Water can, however, be effected by that which is put into the Water. Pollution of any sort can turn a Water spirit malevolent, yet the nature of such a spirit can be changed again with the cleansing of the place. Life added to a source of Water can have a very positive effect. Most ponds and pools will develop their own ecosystems, attracting frogs and fishes and any number of life forms without obvious explanation, but actually contributing fish to a depleted lake or newly made pond is like giving the gift of life to the spirit of the place, and has very positive effects. A small pond constructed within a magical garden and populated with appropriately sized fish can be a very powerful addition to the energy of the place. It also helps the elemental balance of the garden, which would naturally have Earth and Air influences already.

I said in *Spirits of the Earth* that we are creatures of the Earth. This is true, but we are also very much creatures of Water. 70% in fact. Whatever our individual lifestyles may be, we are very much ruled by our emotional natures, even the most 'self-controlled' among us. It is by tapping into the psychic abilities which naturally accompany the emotional side of our nature that we can learn to have psychic vision. It is also in the nature of Water which draws out our emotions, and therefore our aptitude for spiritual vision, which so often makes Water spirits the most easy to see.

5

To See Water Spirits

Water spirits present a rather unique enigma to visual perception in that they are often seen in the reflection of light on or near Water. This makes them more easily seen even to the extent that spontaneous sightings are legendary, yet it also lends an elusive quality to the sighting, leaving the observer unsure whether anything was actually seen or whether it was only a trick of the light.

The cone receptors in the eye (as described in the introduction to this series) can more easily perceive the spectrum of spiritual light when it is amplified by Water reflections, but the forms move and waver, and in most cases, are all too quickly gone before one can adequately discern and assimilate what has been observed. It is often left to imperfect memory and belief to interpret a fleeting image in motion.

There are, of course, exceptions to this phenomena. Like Earth spirits, Water spirits are sometimes known to take form outside of the actual confines of their element. Far too many legends of ghost-lady well spirits, talking fishes and other Water spirits exist to be all the result of collective imagination and superstition. Many of the forms are consistent across cultures, like the seal women and the predilection for serpent-like creatures in the vicinity of specific bodies of Water, most notably at Loch Ness. Water spirits are often bold creatures, unafraid to be seen by humans, yet enjoying the game of hide and seek much as their counterparts among the other elements often play. Many of them are shape changers and

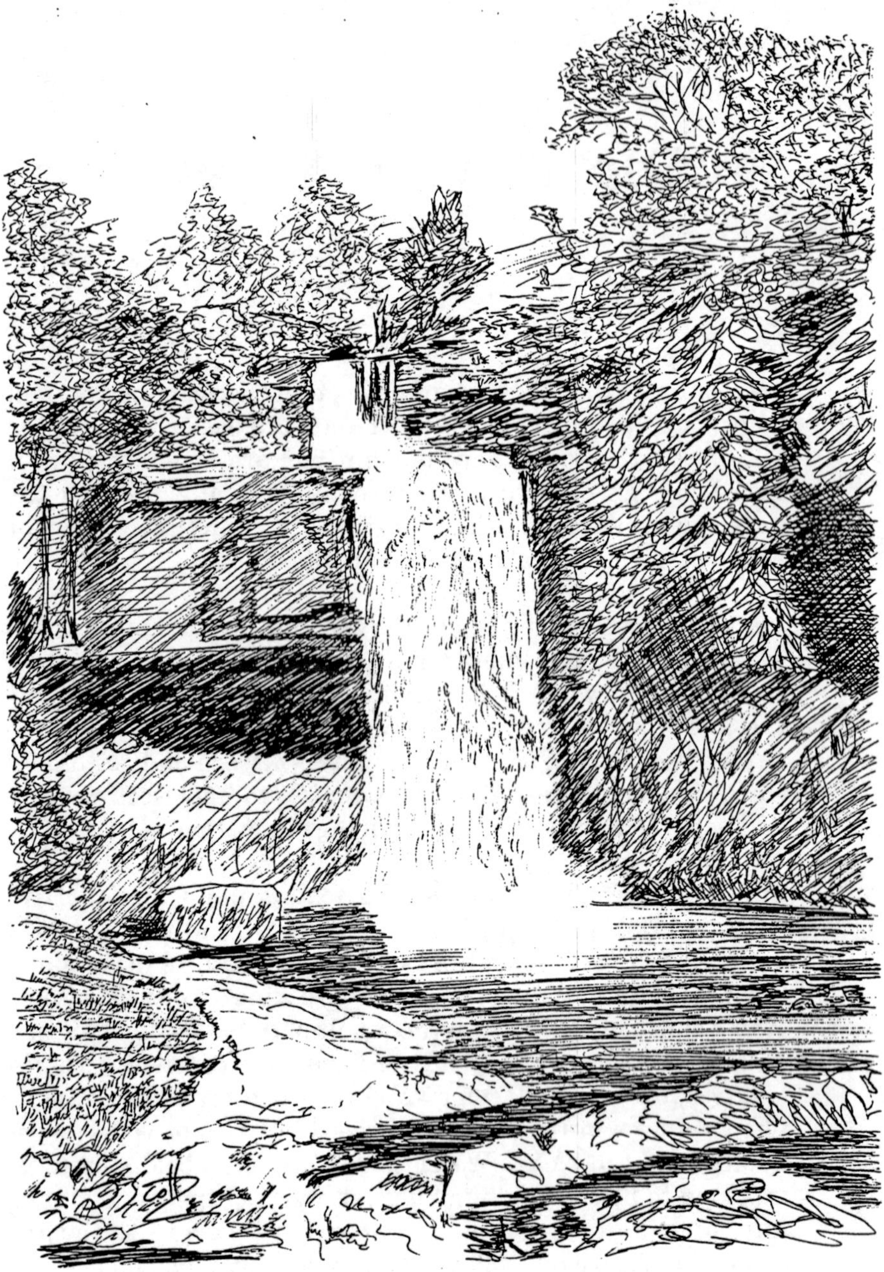

may appear as aquatic animals of some sort. Some of them, particularly spirits of pools, peat bogs and certain seas, actively seek to attract humans for their own purposes. The reader should be careful of these. As is described under some of the entries in chapter 2, there are some Water spirits who seek to consume the life force and may possibly have learned in times gone by to expect the occasional sacrifice.

Apart from obvious bodies of Water and their vicinities, Water spirits may be observed in mirrors, fog, rain, dew or snowbanks. Mirrors and fog are particularly good mediums for scrying and will be spoken of in the divination chapter, but this art can be more effective if one chooses to specifically consult the spirit of the chosen medium. This is one of the reasons that a scrying mirror is traditionally washed with a mixture of vinegar and Water before each use. The mirror, a reflective surface much like Water in a pool, attracts a similar sort of spirit, but the magical washing brings the actual element in contact with the surface and this will assist the working if the assistance of a Water spirit is desired.

Apart from accidental sighting of Water spirits, there are ways to go about actually seeking to observe these spirits which one can practice. Some of them are the stuff of superstition and folklore, others are a simple matter of common sense and understanding of the world of nature spirits.

To Seek Water Spirits In Nature

One example of a superstition of how to go about observing sea spirits is to take a holed stone to the ocean at night, close one eye and look out to sea through the hole with the other eye. This method is based on using a stone which has formed a hole through Water erosion, preferably one found at the seashore, as the stone would have an affinity with the seawater which eroded through it and the actual hole would provide a focus point for observing the required spirit. I cannot say that I have ever personally tried this method, but I can keep an open mind as to its possibilities.

Another method from folklore is to watch the reflection of the Full Moon on the ocean or other body of water. As I've mentioned earlier, the Moon is closely attuned to the natural Waters of the Earth through gravitational pull and is representative of feminine intuition. There is more to this connection than just symbology. Also, the actual light on the Water, besides creating a dance of light and shadow within which the intuitive eye can perceive shapes, will actually attract the creatures of the Water, both physical and spiritual. If you ever observe dolphins playing in their natural habitat at night, you will see them leap and frolic in the streak of Moonlight on the Water. Many creatures of the deep are similarly attracted by the light, although most of them stay under the surface. Water spirits share the playful nature of the dolphin, and, like most spirits, are attracted to the soft light of the Moon more so than the harsh glare of the daytime Sun. Many a sailor throughout history has reported seeing figures, most often ghostly ladies, walking on the surface of the Water in the streak of light given off by the Moon. It may be that some of these ladies were created at the bottom of a rum barrel, but many others have appeared to the sober and sane observer.

The reader of folklore will find many examples worldwide of stories about sightings of Water spirits in various forms as well as superstitions such as the above holed stone method for seeing them. Some of these have been altered by later religious influence, such as the Manx superstition that a child whose eye touches water in baptism has no chance of becoming second sighted. For the less superstitious and more practical seeker, the key is to remember that any source of Water, even dew on the grass, is a potential wellspring of Water spirit activity. One only has to learn the knack for catching a glimpse of movement on the edges of the reflection of light and shadow which characterizes the medium of Water, and then to trust the evidence of one's own eyes.

As with Earth spirits, it is possible to choose a place to specifically seek Water spirits, perhaps even befriend them and allow the place of Water to become special in some way to you. This is most often done with ponds or other small bodies of Water, which are preferable to most people than attempting this with a fast moving Water source such as a river. Ponds are places which breed a spirit of calm, which may also be said of gently trickling streams.

It is best if the chosen place is unlikely to be invaded by passers-by, yet as in all nature treks, one should follow safety procedures and avoid natural dangers. A Water pool in an African jungle may be beautifully isolated from human interruption, but it could get ugly when the lions come down to drink! There are some very calm swamps in Australia which are teaming with spiritual life, but I don't fancy explaining to a crocodile that I just came to meditate with the spirits. In America, isolated streams may be frequented by bears or mountain lions, not to mention water moccasins or other poisonous snakes. I love animals, but there are some that are best left undisturbed and claiming a source of Water for a meditation spot may infringe on the natural wildlife of the area. Here in the U.K., we don't have many large or dangerous animals to worry about, but we must still consider the habitat of smaller animals when choosing to visit a natural place where humans are otherwise infrequent intruders.

As described in *Spirits of the Earth*, the method for attuning to the spirits of your chosen place is to begin by just sitting and listening for the first few visits. The seeker should visit the place as often as possible, but do nothing to interfere with anything in the location. The local wildlife, as well as the location spirits, will become accustomed to your presence eventually and the place will begin to feel very natural and welcoming. Always eat something as a natural form of grounding after each visit, but it is best not to do so until leaving the place, and absolutely nothing should be left behind (apart from a biodegradable offering).

This process sounds easy, but it requires patience and fortitude. The feeling of the place may go through many stages before reaching the state of absolute calm which is required to proceed. If the seeker is tested by a feeling of hostility, the decision will have to be made as to whether the spirits of the place are really unwilling to tolerate this human intrusion, or whether they will get used to the new presence and assimilate it.

Once the seeker's presence is accepted and welcomed by the location spirits, it is time to deal directly with the source of Water. Gazing across the surface of a pool or the edges of a stream may lead to immediate sightings, or may only begin by peripheral glimpses of reflection and movement. Depending on the form of the Water, it may be possible to actually enter into the element and repeat the attuning exercise within the Water itself, but again the seeker is advised to consider safety. Very cold Water or fast currents are real dangers, and some places are prone to sudden flooding. Choose your place wisely and keep an eye on the weather!

In *Spirits of the Earth*, the seeker of Earth spirits is advised to unfocus the eyes and use the peripheral vision to try to see spiritual auras. A similar method is used with Water spirits, but there are some distinct differences. First of all, the Water spirit may be lurking within the Water itself and the only result one will get from looking into a body of Water with slightly unfocused vision is to see a blur of reflection. The method can be used to look at the edges of the Water, which is more likely to bring results in a stream than a pond as Water spirits often play among the rocks and natural plant life which grows along the edge of the Water, but within the Water itself, a different approach is required.

Water spirits are most easily seen between extremes of light and darkness, so dawn and dusk are the best times to look for them. Any source of Water will have some light reflection, even on a dark night. Bright sunlight reflected off of Water can be blinding. To seek visual perception of a spirit within the Water, the methods change again depending on whether one seeks them on the surface or is prepared to plunge one's head into the Water itself. Seeking visual perception of Water spirits on the surface is accomplished by moving the eyes constantly over the reflections and looking with the peripheral vision. The eye will catch movements, even in a perfectly calm pool, but many of these are ripples of Water or insects moving about. The seeker may be astounded at the degree of movement which can be perceived at this point. It is a matter of practice to learn to differentiate the ethereal movement of a Water spirit from the ordinary movements of aquatic and insect life which catch the eye all too easily, but the contrast becomes obvious once a first spirit sighting is accomplished.

Beneath the surface, there is much less distraction from fliting bugs, frogs and blowing leaves. The animal movements are more easily recognizable as little fishes swim about (sometimes big ones too!), but visibility may be very poor depending on the clarity of the Water itself and the degree of light available. In conditions of very poor visibility, a diving mask may be helpful. However, the natural distortion of vision which occurs in Water can be an advantage. There is no need to unfocus the eyes underwater and the natural tendency to flit the eyes about in search of clear vision is ideal for seeking the movements of Water spirits.

There are two important things to remember when seeking Water spirits under the surface. One is that you must breath and it's no good trying to duck under and keep coming up for Air. This prohibits any chance of settling into a visual field as the interruptions would have to be very frequent. A snorkle or even proper diving equipment may well be in order, but do not go diving into deep Water without proper training. If you go diving with a 'buddy' as is required by safety rules, it would be best to recruit a friend who shares your quest, or at least an interest.

The other thing to keep in mind is that this is *their* realm. You are an intruder. They may welcome you, but they may just as easily resent the intrusion, even if the location spirits above the Water line have accepted you. Read some of the tales in the books included in the bibliography and you will find many stories of drownings attributed to Water spirits.

Don't forget to leave something for the Water spirits, as well as for the Earth spirits of the location when leaving. A bit of cake sprinkled on the surface of the Water is ideal, as it helps to feed the fishes. Just a little given to a nearby tree completes the offering. As explained in the chapter on sacred wells, many ponds and pools are attended by a nearby tree and/or standing stone. A natural place may well have a tree nearby which can serve this function.

Another thing to remember is that the place should not be unduly interfered with. If your chosen place is a domestic pond, cleaning it up periodically is perfectly acceptable and should please the resident spirits. If, on the other hand, it is a wild stream or pool, it is best left to nature unless it is overcrowded with dead leaves or has been polluted. In general, nature knows how to look after itself.

Those who live near a fast moving river or the ocean may naturally wish to seek Water spirits in these places despite my suggestion that a calmer location is easiest. For these people, the fact that they live near these places creates an exception and the same general methods already described are fine. Their constant proximity to these more active Watery places creates an attunement which compensates for the seemingly violent nature of the moving Water. Having lived near an ocean during much of my life, I am well aware that waves or torrents which may seem intimidating to a visitor to the area can actually have a very calming effect on a local resident who will have assimilated the natural rhythms of ocean or river.

To See Invited Water Spirits

As with the other elements, Water spirits can be invited into the element, despite the fact that they will already exist there, as a way of introducing oneself to them. This is especially effective with newly made sources of Water, such as a constructed pond, where the ritual can act as a form of welcome. Some examples for invitation rituals will be included in the appendix, but I strongly recommend that the reader construct a personal ritual for this if possible. Water, the element of emotion, requires ritual which flows from the heart rather than from a page. A pond which has been constructed or cleaned up will already have become personal to the one who has done the work, a few words of welcoming for the spirits of this new Water source should come easily if it isn't forced. A simple statement such as, "*I welcome the spirits of Water to this pond and invite their magic to reign here forever more*", delivered with the love of a labour accomplished, are quite sufficient.

Inviting Water spirits into a particular stretch of ocean or an age old lake, river or stream may seem redundant in the extreme as the Water spirits will of course be long established. In this situation, the invitation can actually be reversed. After all, it is you, the human, who is the new entity in such a place. An invitation can read as an offer of friendship, effectively inviting oneself to become a part of the place, if the established Water spirits so desire and accept the offer. This is one circumstance where it is very wise to remember that the Water spirits were here long before you. There is no law which guarantees that they must accept your presence. It is not the right of even a very talented magician to impose one's own will on a place of nature or to try to subdue the spiritual inhabitants. Water, calm as it may seem in its undisturbed state, is a very powerful element and the spirits of Water are more formidable than one might remember when gazing into a calm pool. Respect them.

Spontaneous Sightings

As I mentioned at the beginning of this chapter, spontaneous sightings of Water spirits are legendary. They happen more frequently and in more bizarre circumstances than with any other element. The observer may not always recognize what has occurred, yet they will know that something unusual certainly has taken place.

Obviously, it is not possible to seek out a spontaneous occurrence. They just happen. An encounter with a Water spirit can be recognized by a particularly 'otherworldly' feeling about the experience or the entity which is encountered. It is a strange feeling of calm, and of 'oldness', which accompanies the usual feeling of something odd. People have described encounters with Water spirits as seeming as if they occurred in a dream. Showing an interest in Water spirits is very likely to result in some form of encounter sooner rather than later. As I said before, Water spirits do not fear humans, although they are particularly playful. One must always remember though that their games are not always nice. If ever the words "*be careful what you wish for*" have been appropriate, it is when one chooses to invite Water spirits into an act of deliberate magic.

6

Water Spirits In Natural Magic

Bringing a Water spirit into an act of natural magic is not at all difficult. In fact, if one performs such an act near any body of Water, it is highly likely that the spirits of that body of Water will participate, invited or not.

Water, by its very nature, seduces and lures the human spirit into a magical state of mind. It has a natural calming effect which is very conducive to attaining trance state. The simple act of having a bath or shower can relax tension. Any form of meditation or contemplation performed near a large body of Water is assisted by the enticement of calm which exudes from the Water itself. Imagine then, how much more effective an act of magic may be if it's performance is enhanced by a deliberate invitation to the Water spirits and an active request for them to participate.

Water spirits exist anywhere that Water may be found, indoors or outdoors. Water spells performed indoors may be performed with common Water from the tap, which may be drunk or used for cooking in kitchen spells, or Water in the bath or even the shower may be used for cleansing or other Water related spells. An incantation to obtain a state of total relaxation performed during a shower can be very effective indeed. A spontaneous spell done while relaxing in the bath can be just as effective as one which is deliberately set up in advance.

68

Some people may keep sources of Water indoors such as an electric fountain or a simple bowl of Water kept for scrying or other spells. Water from sources such as sacred wells may be kept bottled, ready for use in one's working space or Temple.

Outdoors, there are of course many more possibilities. One may feel compelled to perform an act of magic by simply being in the vicinity of certain streams, rivers, ponds or the seaside. Water spirit spells can be very useful when swimming, or especially if one finds oneself in unexpected difficulties such as sinking in a bog, caught in undergrowth in a lake or even lost in the ocean after a disaster. There are many tales of sailors who are rescued by dolphins after a shipwreck and taken to a floating object or even in some cases a nearby island. Some have told tales of being similarly rescued by mermaids, although these tales are often put down to hallucination. One wonders....

Water spells are commonly used for cleansing and purification, accessing the subconscious and stabilizing the emotions. Water is fluid, constantly changing, and these qualities must be kept in mind when performing Water spells of any kind. Water is representative of pleasure, friendship, marriage, fertility, happiness, healing, sleep, dreaming and psychic acts. Spells which concern any of these things may well be appropriate for the Water element. Some, such as fertility and healing, may also require or be appropriate to another element. It depends rather a lot on the approach which is intended.

There is an old belief that Water is particularly powerful when the morning sun first shines on it, which may be at the basis for the name *Brightwell* which adorns many place names and ancient wells. A simple spell can be performed by simply mentally projecting a sigil onto the reflection of either the Sun or the Moon on the Water surface, allowing oneself to relax into the meditative state which is all too easy to lose oneself in while contemplating the Water's surface, allowing oneself to slip into the depths of trance. This state is very conducive to sleep, which could be inconvenient outdoors, but a form of the same method can be performed indoors over a bowl of Water, positioned to catch the Moonlight through the window. The spirit of the Water can be called to aid in the purpose, but it is recommended that this form of spell is restricted to calmer purposes as a very active spell or one that involves strong emotions could be disturbing or even offensive to the Water spirit.

Water Spells In Folk Magic

Water is perhaps the most commonly used element in folk magic. It is often used in its cleansing capacity, both physically and symbolically. Old superstitions commonly reflect practical health precautions such as the belief that one should never drink Water which has stood in a glass overnight. It is believed that such Water would then be possessed by demonic forces, or that fairies would have taken the essence from the Water as they are believed to do with milk and food offerings, but in fact these superstitions date from a time when Water left standing may have been contaminated with such things as typhoid or influenza germs in days when such diseases were epidemic and often incurable by the medicines known at the time.

Some other superstitions regarding Water are less dire in origin and intent. One classic belief is that if on the first of May, one rubs the morning dew into one's face, it will keep the skin young looking. Stone magic can be mixed with Water magic by dipping stones in Water to conduct their magical properties, followed by drinking the Water. A form of sigil magic is performed by using an object to symbolize a desire which is then tossed or placed into Water. A similar folk spell is performed by drawing a symbol to represent something one wishes to 'cleanse away' from one's life on a stone or other object, then tossing it into Water, preferably a running source, to wash away the affliction. In modern Pagan groups, Water is often used symbolically in Earth cleansing rituals.

Water itself does not have to be present for all magical workings, but can be symbolized by things which are given to us from the sea or other natural bodies of Water. It is a common belief that a shell placed at the entrance of a house ensures that good luck will enter it. Shells are frequently used in ritual of all sorts and have been fascinating objects to humans, especially children, for as long as we have existed. Conch shells produce a loud trump when blown which makes for a good opening to a sea ritual, but can be used symbolically in other rituals as well. Holed stones which are given up by the sea are also considered to be lucky.

Much of weather lore concerns the warning signals for rain, more so than for snow, hail, or other celestial phenomena. The following rhyme is from tree lore, and is considered to be a seasonal guide or predictor of rainfall. It is based on the order in which trees blossom for the season;

Ash before oak,
We're in for a soak.
Oak before ash,
We're in for a splash.

Magic By The Seaside

Magic of the ocean is possibly the most commonly practised among ordinary people. Fishermen and sailors have given us centuries of folk beliefs as well as legends and folktales. Much of the ways of the sea are based on the physical effects of the tides which are closely linked to the phases of the Moon. Tides work in approximately twelve hour cycles, but are correlated to the twenty-eight day cycles of the Moon as well. An incoming tide (called Flow) correlates to a waxing

Moon, while the outgoing tide (Ebb) correlates to the waning Moon. In the Charles Dickens novel David Copperfield, the character Mr. Jarvis dies as the tide goes out which is predicted by the onlookers. This is a reflection of a common folk belief that the spirit goes out with the tide.

Magical tools may be brought along for acts of sea magic, or objects may be gathered at the seaside for spontaneous rituals. Quite often no implements are required at all for this sort of magic, as the ocean and its relation to the spirit of the magician can be quite enough.

High tide is a good time for sea magic as it correlates to the Full Moon, but low tide is not frequently used in magic as it correlates to the New Moon. Although there are situations where a New Moon is appropriate in magic, the low tide is a time of low power. It can however be a good time for meditation, introspection, and seeking information from past lives.

In any given seaside location, there are two high tides and two low tides in a twenty-four hour period. You can chart the times for these tides from information given in local papers, libraries, and sports/fishing stores. From a practical point of view, it is particularly important to be aware of tides if you are actually performing your ritual on a stretch of beach, as you could find your Altar suddenly being swallowed up in the flow or even find yourself trapped against a rocky cliffside as the beach disappears beneath the rising tide. One must remember that time frequently runs differently when in ritual trance. More than one person has suddenly found the waves swirling around their ankles unexpectedly while their thoughts were distracted. Many years ago, such an incident was related to me by a friend who had been lost in magical musings on a beach in Devon, which resulted in a rather shaky climb up a ladder on a cliffside which had been permanently fixed there for just such an occasion, as this particular cove was given to sudden immersion which had claimed more than one unwary tourist.

The sea, despite its salt, sand and other apparent 'impurities' is very good for cleansing, purifying and trance rituals. One simple spell for spiritual cleansing in the sea is to let the waves splash over you and make a simple statement such as, "*I am renewed*". An easy way to obtain trance is to sit on the beach and listen to the natural rhythms of the waves crashing. This can be done with eyes closed, or a different sort of trance state may be achieved by watching the reflection of the Full Moon on the ocean and projecting a magical wish into the wavering forms in the reflection of light. With some practice, one can use the release of energy in the crashing waves to magnify power for any spell.

A simple sigil spell may be performed by writing the need or a symbol which represents the desire into wet sand near the tide line during flow and chanting a simple ritual over the space as the tide washes the image away, but remember that the tide is coming in, so you'll want to use this for a positive spell, one that brings something into your life rather than something which requires release.

Chanting A Water Spell

One of the oldest images of witchcraft is that of a woman (usually a hag) chanting while stirring some sort of brew in a cauldron. This is, in fact, a very effective spell method, although the folktale images are usually distorted.

Water stirred in a pot on its own creates a visual vortex, a focal point which can lead to magical trance. A cooking spell which wishes goodness to come from the food may only involve a light trance, but other spells, whether performed in the traditional cauldron or a common saucepan, can use the method for much deeper levels of trance which may be required for magic of greater difficulty. Symbolic ingredients can be added to the Water during the course of the spell, especially herbs which may be used for their specific scents as well as symbolism. I have yet to meet a witch or magician who actually uses eye of newt, toe of frog or bat wings as in some classic stories, but items which symbolize the objective of the spell are certainly appropriate.

The cauldron method may be used for charging binding spells, luck spells and many other purposes which may involve submersing a talisman or symbolic construction of some form into the 'magical stew'.

Water spells can have terrific force behind them if one evokes the more potentially violent aspects of Water, but in general, working with Water spirits brings an effect of serene tranquillity which far surpasses the spiritually calming reaction which one generally has to working with spirits of other elements. In fact, the magician must be a bit wary of slipping into depression if there is prolonged work specifically with Water. If this should occur, an uplifting ritual involving Air or Fire is strongly recommended. Most often, balancing the elements is best but there are always exceptions where a focus on a specific element is appropriate.

Water promotes spiritual cleansing. Often, it is the emotions which are subject to this process. The spirits of Water reflect this association with emotion in their nature and are generally inclined to react when they are called, and sometimes when they are not. Water draws the practitioner of magic deep into the realms of their own strong emotions, sometimes into places of darkness where many fear to tread. It is this quality of Water spirit magic which begs for the controls which are made present in an act of formal ritual.

7

Water Spirits In Ritual

Water spirits may be called into ritual as guardians, for various purposes attributed to Water or as spiritual entities required for a ritual which is specifically focused on Water. A standard ritual Altar set-up will usually include a chalice to represent Water, but this is most often filled with wine rather than Water itself. For the calling of guardians or a representation of the element in a balanced ritual, using a symbolic tool, such as a shell, is fine. However, for a ritual specific to Water to be most effective, a source of actual Water is highly recommended, even if one chooses to create a thought-form elemental to perform the purpose intended.

A Water spirit can be invited into an item to represent Water for your Altar for most purposes. This can be the traditional chalice, or something more akin to the element itself, probably something which has come to you through a source of Water. Items which are given up by the sea are particularly appropriate for ritual tools representing Water, as the sea is the *'Great Source'* and largest body of Water on our planet. Shells are an obvious choice, and are symbolic of the sea gods. Long spiral shells represent the god force while rounded shells such as cowries represent the goddess. These are often used to represent the goddess on a standard Altar, as Water is a feminine element. Holed stones found by the shore are also excellent representations, but can be difficult to find. Any item found in Water which 'speaks' to you can be made appropriate for a Water quarter representation.

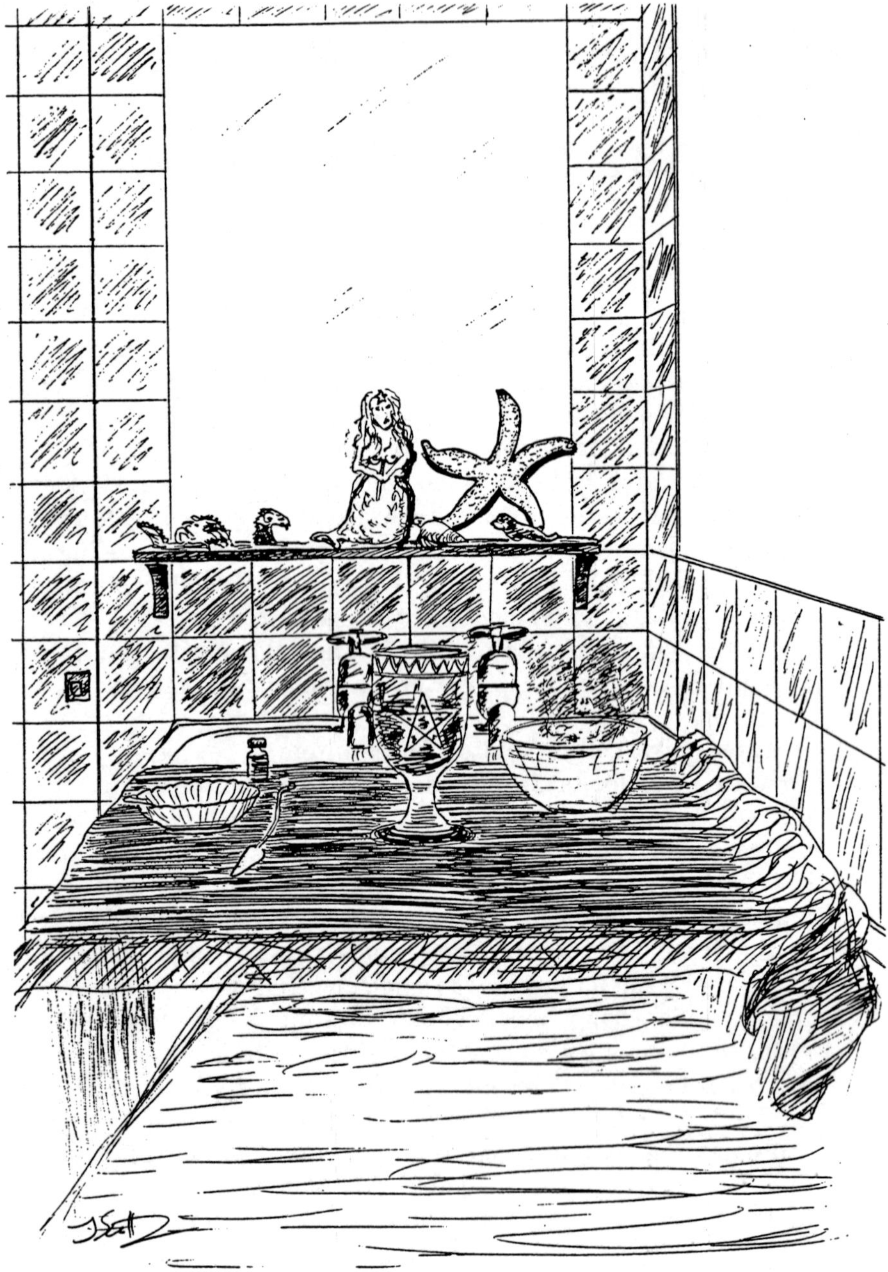

Calling Quarters

Calling the quarter for Water in a ritual which includes all of the elements involves rather a lot of internal drama rather than external, as Water is representative of emotion. Conch shells, as mentioned in the previous chapter, make excellent trumpets for announcing the opening of a ritual, but opening a quarter with the trump of a conch shell is probably too dramatic for private rituals to which one may not wish to draw attention, although a large public ritual could benefit from such an attention getter. Usually, a simple invitation to the spirits of Water to participate in the ritual is sufficient, but an internal emotional appeal to them is what will bring the desired response. Without the element of emotion, a ritual quickly becomes stagnant and inflexible, no more than a group of people reading words from a script. It is the element of Water which acts as a fluid medium to carry the spirit of magic forward, through emotional responses of the participants. The person designated to call the quarter for Water has a rather heavy responsibility in this.

Water is an element of constant change, and it is the progressive flow of the mutable stuff of the world of Spirit which causes change to occur in accordance with Will, as that nice Mr. Crowley put it. The importance of the element of Water to any ritual is as clear as pure Water itself.

If you choose to keep a representation for Water in a Temple quarter, it is likely to be the West quarter decorated in shades of blue and sea-green as that is the direction used in nearly all systems, including the Hereditary system. In this Water is consistent, which is an odd quality of Water. It is the element of change, yet its basic qualities are consistent throughout the changes. Even if conditions such as freezing or vaporising transmute Water into a solid or gaseous form, left to rest in normal conditions it will return to its original fluid form. Water can be knocked about by tides, items entered into it, wind or any number of things, yet left to rest it will calm itself at a slow but steady rate until it is perfectly still. Water in all of its forms constantly seeks to compensate for any amount of interference, even in situations such as the sea where the interference is never ending.

It is through learning to shape the use of emotional energy very much in the pattern of the actions of natural Water that the astute magician can learn to harness its power. To call an emotion at will or to calm one's emotions when required by outside circumstances are more difficult tasks than they may sound, but are inherent lessons which any magician must learn to master if one's magic is to have any control. This ability goes far beyond the necessary state for opening the Water quarter for a ritual, but is a requirement for the effective use of spirit magic in any situation, Water rituals most of all.

For the basic opening of the Water quarter, many systems have specific wording such as, "*Hail to the guardians of the West..*" etc. For those who are bound by these systems, it may be possible to add a bit onto the end such as, "*...and we invite* (name of spirit), *spirit of this chalice* (or shell, or other item) *representative of* (or given from) *the Great Source of Water, to be guardian of the West in this and all our celebrations of the goddess, so shall it be.*" Exact wording is open to individual or group preferences of course.

Another possibility is to perform an elemental dedication ritual as described in Spirits of the Earth, which names spirits of all of the elements and invites them to participate in all future rituals done by that group, or individual. In this ritual, the person who will speak the invitation for Water steps to the West quarter (in turn) and speaks the name given to the spirit, or simply "*Spirit of the Water...*", then continues: "*We invite you to join our rites and our circle, to be as one with us, and to be forever our guardian of the West. In return, we ask that you help us to be at one with the Great Source of*

Water, to convey the intent of our magic through the mutable stuff of Spirit, and to lend us your your power in matters of the emotions and all that is represented by the element of Water, if such is your judgement. Let it be so." (or *"so mote it be."*)

Those who are free to make up their own wordings for ritual openings are certainly encouraged to do so. Examples will be included in the appendix for opening, closing and inviting a Water spirit into an item to represent Water, but the important thing with Water rituals is to speak from the heart and put plenty of emotional content into the appeal or invitation.

Water Rituals Out Of Doors

Once a ritual implement is established, one may wish to take it to an outdoor location in order to perform a formal ritual with the benefit of a natural source of Water, or one may even wish to enter the Water for the purpose of performing the ritual. Obviously there are practical considerations to this. A calm source of Water such as a pond can easily have an Altar set up in shallow Water, or even laid out on a float of some sort. The problem with this is that there is always a danger that the float could easily be disturbed and all of your ritual equipment sink to the bottom! Among the breaking waves in the ocean is of course no place to set up things which you don't wish to lose, although the seaside is perfectly appropriate. The reader will have to decide whether it is worth bringing along such items, or whether it may be preferable to call on the location spirits, combining natural magic with formal ritual.

As with other elements, location spirits should be asked for permission before performing a ritual in *their* place, even if it is a place which you often use for this purpose or frequent for other reasons. A particularly strong ritual could be performed by bringing along your Temple implements and also inviting the local spirits to join in. Water spirits are just as full of fun as other elemental spirits, although they 'feel' different and can give the impression of being very deep and serious. Remember that 'joy' is one of the strongest emotions, and can be invoked as part of an opening for a Water ritual which may include a bit of splashing around. Again, be sure that your implements are secure, or that you are prepared to go diving for them.

Water Spirits For A Specific Task

Besides cleansing, purification and anything involving the emotions, Water rituals may be used for any purpose which makes use of the subconscious. In fact, nearly any purpose which magic may be used for can be approached through Water. It is a matter of approach and attitude. Like crystals, Water carries electromagnetic energy, but Water is fluid and although it can be contained to an extent, it has a tendency to seep or to find other ways to free itself from constricting parameters. This is something to bear in mind when working with Water spirit energies.

Some purposes are very appropriate to Water rituals such as seeking pleasure, friendship, marriage or happiness in any form. Also, spells for sleep, lucid dreaming, or performing psychic acts are appropriate to Water. Sleep spells in particular are able to benefit from the use of a Water spirit, as these spirits naturally wish to draw one into the depths of the subconscious, but caution should be exercised as this tendency could go too far and one does wish to awaken eventually. Some spells for fertility or healing may be approached by Water. Examples for all of these will be included in the appendix.

Some people believe that Water which is kept in coloured jars takes on the corresponding quality of the colour used, and that drinking the Water brings that quality into oneself. This can be done with ordinary tap Water, but some purists believe that pure spring Water is required for best effect. Some forms of negative magic are also appropriate to Water. Cursing for example, is something which requires a great deal of emotion and is from the feminine realm of magic, but this association with the element of Water should serve as a warning to all that this sort of magic can be very unpredictable. It is very easy to lose control of parameters in negative magic, and for that reason alone is not to be done lightly.

A very simple form of sigil spell can be used for most magical purposes. It is performed by saving a piece of driftwood from a visit to the seaside. One carves designs as for most sigil spells, representing the desire, then charges the sigil which can be subsequently destroyed in a bonfire, or thrown into the sea as the tide goes out. The main difference between this ritual and the one in the previous chapter where the sigil is drawn in wet sand is that the driftwood can be taken home to construct a more detailed sigil and to perform a more elaborate charging ritual.

The ocean is very cooperative in general in providing treasures from its depths that we may collect without disturbing any form of ecological balance. Inland sources of Water may be less forthcoming, but it is a simple matter to take an item to a chosen source of Water, wash it, and perform a dedication ritual to attune it to the source of Water. Much of the magic of Water works within the realm of symbolism, just as our minds translate our subconscious thought patterns into symbols in dreams. The use of symbols of any kind, and particularly in the most abstract sense, is very appropriate to Water. With that in mind, perhaps it would be appropriate to present the reader with some abstract and symbolic magical correspondences.

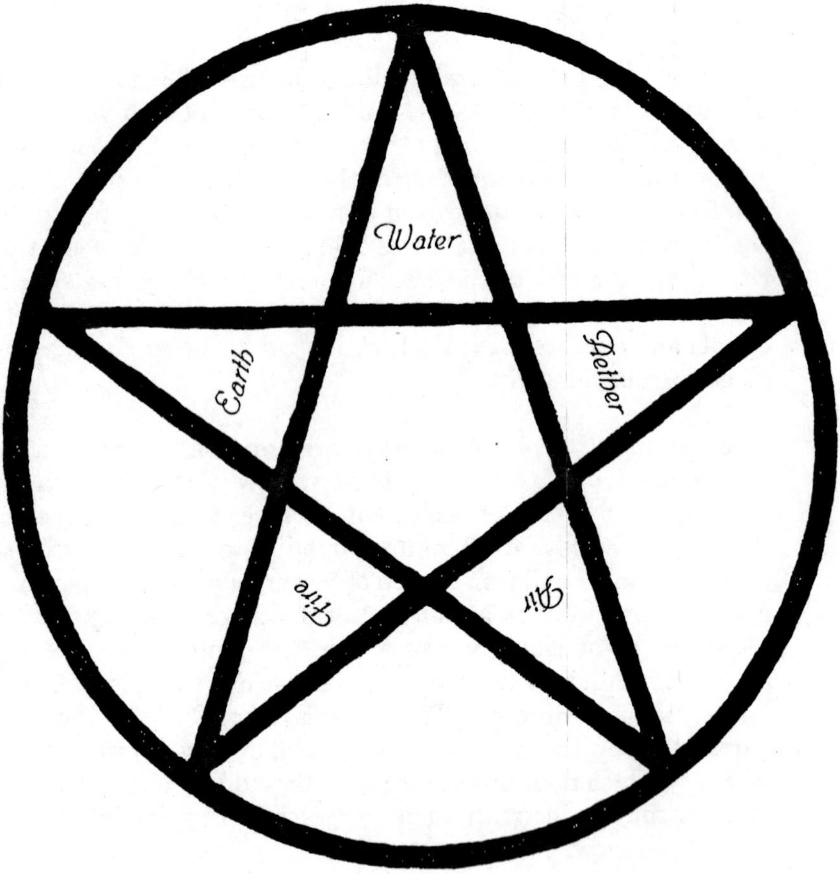
Water
Earth
Aether
Fire
Air

8

Correspondences

I have said in the previous volumes of this series that systems of correspondences have little or no meaning to elemental spirits and are primarily used for our own benefit to form associations between one thing and another. This is true. However, it is here in the realm of Water spirits that the value of symbols and associations to the subconscious mind are explained and absorbed into active magical practice.

Water is the element of the subconscious. This is the realm where magic transmutes intent into new possibilities, where they may take active form. The "appropriate frame of mind" for magic which I mentioned in *Spirits of the Earth* is essentially a psychological state wherein we are opened to the messages of the subconscious and can meld that which comes from the depths of our minds to conscious thought and even to communication with the world of Spirit, or to sublimate our wishes into that subconscious realm where the magic is allowed to form into a vibrational force which can effect conditions outside of ourselves.

Water is associated with the Deep blue of the sea, with the direction West, and with the Autumn season. It is also associated with symbolism in all its forms and with the world of dreams.

What are dreams, but symbols of our own sub-conscious' making? Books about dream symbolism are popular sellers, yet these subconscious symbols are unique to every person and cannot be categorized as easily as many dream dictionaries would suggest. Symbols may mean very different things to different people.

Some symbols recur frequently in different cultures. Spirals are one of the most common representations of any form of energy, including the life force, and are similar to the labyrinth designs which appear in many world wide locations. Often it is speculated by archaeologists that these labyrinth designs represent the mysteries of life, which associates them with fertility. Stars with varying numbers of points are also frequently found in widely diverse cultures, and great significance is attached to the number of points and the specific construction of each form of star. For example, the five pointed star used in the pentagram is representative of the five elements, including Spirit, and is also representative of Man. Sometimes the symbol appears with a picture of a man overlaid, his arms and legs outstretched to fill the points below his head which occupies the top point. The Seal of Solomon, which is commonly used in Hebrew symbolism, is constructed of two triangles, one pointing up and the other pointing down. These triangles represent the concept of *"as above, so below"* which appears in many religions and magical philosophies.

Some of the most potent magic is accomplished when the magician has in mind an abstract idea of what is desired, and is able to leave the subconscious in control of the act of magic in order to allow the symbolic work done within what Aleister Crowley called *"True Will"* to manifest into a result which is decided unconsciously. This requires a great deal of trust in oneself and in one's magic, as this sort of work is accomplished through the realms of natural chaos. Working with Water spirits can be very beneficial in symbolic work as the conscious intent creates parameters which the Water spirits can work within while performing their own often chaotic exertions.

Some systems of symbols are well known and often used such as the Wiccan common terms for elemental spirits;

>Earth - Gnomes
>
>Air - Sylphs
>
>Fire - Salamanders
>
>Water - Undines

Other systems are less often used, and more likely to play a role in more subtle symbology in ritual or in personal associations such as the following Celtic animal correspondences;

Name	Animal	Cardinal Direction
Cernunnos	Stag	East
Epona	White Mare	South
Mona	Sacred Cow	West
Artor	Great Bear	North

In this system, there is also an Aetherial association with the wolf, which leads the Shaman into the 'otherworlds'. These animals are considered to be the Guardians of Albion. The symbology may be used directly by some groups, but is more often something which works on the intuitional level.

Animal spirit identification is intuitional by nature. It is known to have been used in tribal societies in many parts of the world. Unlike actual shapeshifting which is associated with Fire, animal spirit identification is a method of accessing the subconscious by aligning one's thoughts with the nature of the chosen animal as it is understood by the Shaman, through its habits and whatever experience the Shaman has of the animal, which clears the conscious mind and allows the more basic instincts to rise to the level of control. This might also be said of pathworking, although this is usually a guided process which turns over control to an outside entity. Both methods work with theta brain waves, and both have some potential for bringing forth some of the hidden aspects of ourselves which can be difficult to confront.

Semiotics is the science of signs and symbols. As most readers will know, the Chalice is a common symbol for Water as an element. Some other known symbols which are used in the construction of talismans as well as other purposes are;

ACORN
Vigour, youthfulness, royalty, prolonged effort preceding perfect achievement.

ANCHOR
Hope, safe anchorage, stability in a changing situation.

ANKH (Egyptian)
Creative power, bringing knowledge, abundance and power.

ARROWHEAD
Protection against evil.

BAT
Health, wealth, love of virtue, long life, happiness.

BELL
Protection against evil.

CADUCEUS
The wand of Mercury or Hermes - duality, balance of health, eloquence of speech.

CORNUCOPIA
Plenty, good fortune, prosperity and fruitfulness.

CRESCENT
Protection from lunacy, success in love, happiness in motherhood, the divine feminine principle.

CROSS
Protection against evil, balanced energies.

EAGLE
Sharp sight, good fortune, dignity and respect. Used to attract the favour of those in high places.

EYE
All seeing, very powerful symbol in Egyptian magic.

FAN
Authority and power, protection and safety when worn.

FATIMA'S HAND
Hospitality, generosity power and divine providence.

FROG
Egyptian symbol of life, symbol of health and strength, particularly recovery after illness.

LADDER
To overcome difficulties on the Earth plane.

LADYBIRD
Good fortune and wealth.

LIZARD
Good fortune and good eyesight.

OWL
Wisdom and learning.

PALM
Triumph of good over temptation.

PHOENIX
Renewal, regeneration.

PINE CONE
Abundant benefits, health, power, wealth.

SALMON
Endurance, wisdom, increase and expansion.

SCARAB
Creation, health, strength and virility.

SERPENT
Regeneration, cycle of creation and destruction.

SHIP
Safe passage.

SPIDER
'Spinning' wealth, shrewdness and foresight in business.

STORK
Good weather, a birth.

VULTURE
Egyptian symbol for healing, power and wisdom.

On the following pages are some symbols which are used in magic, talisman construction and sometimes for personal adornment, either as jewellery, tatoos or embroidery on clothing. Also included are some examples of magic squares as well as seals and sigils for specific entities which require further explanation, but I will save that for *Spirits of the Aether*. I include them here for their visual significance.

5-pointed star

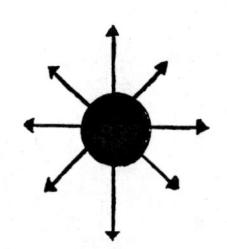

Chaosphere

Pentagram

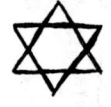

Seal of Soloman

Sigil of the Gateway

Sigillum Dei AEmeth

Seal of Babalon
A∴ A∴

Yin/Yang

Labyrinth

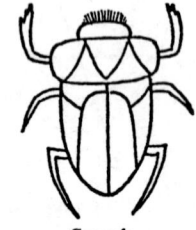

Scarab

Baphomet

Thor's Hammer

Ankh

Spiral

Earth

Air

Spirit

Fire

Water

or

The Seal of Baal

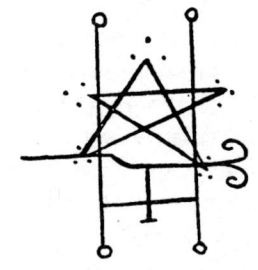

The Seal of Astaroth

Moon · Kamea 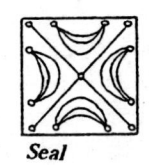 · Seal  · Spirit - Chashmodai

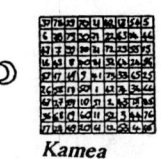

SEALS AS DRAWN BY A.E. WAITE

91

The Fryske (or water witches) are known for the symbol which still appears on many canal boats; a six spike wheel design. It is a religious symbol for them which attaches significance to the colours of the different spikes. Their rituals usually include the invokation of an elemental and the placing of objects of appropriate colours in the appropriate directional quarter. These colours use a system which the Fryske have in common with the Druids. The correspondences are as follows;

North	Earth	Black	Winter	Midnight	New Moon
East	Air	Red	Spring	Sunrise	First Quarter
South	Fire	White	Summer	Midday	Full Moon
West	Water	Grey	Autumn	Sunset	Last Quarter

Music has been mentioned in *Spirits of the Air* as sounds are generally associated with Air. However, music must also be included here as certain music directly effects the emotions. Different people respond differently to various forms of music. Many people respond in particular to music which combines primal drumming with the elusive quality of the flute and/or the haunting strains of the violin, yet there are many other responses to the spectrum of musical effects which are obtainable through everything from ancient instruments to modern technological synthesizers.

One musical instrument in particular seems to have an almost universal appeal. That is the human voice. Again, people respond differently to different sorts of voices, but one way or another, they generally do respond. Have you ever wondered why a powerful singing voice with just the right amount of vibratto can make you feel anything, any emotion, as if it could tear into your soul and shape your emotions at the will of the song itself? For some, this response is brought about by old singers like Bing Crosby, while for others it may come from Janis Joplin, modern bands like Marilyn Manson, folk music, pop bands...there are any number of possibilities.

There are still some who prefer the instrumental effects in jazz or classical music, or even the weird effects exhibited in industrial music, yet by and large, the human voice has the ability to penetrate beyond the simple enjoyment of music and reach into the emotional response centres with an intensity that can only be compared to the profound reaction which one might have to supreme love or sorrow. This is a power which should never be taken for granted, yet may be used in ritual with very creative results.

Symbols, visual, audio or stemming from any of the senses, are important to magic. They are used to access the subconscious for both ritual and for divination, to align ourselves with those energies with which we choose to associate, and can be very important in the formation of thought-form elementals.

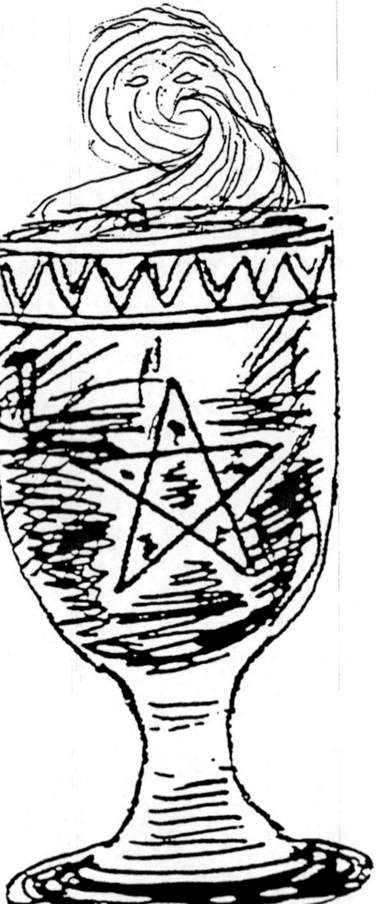

9

Water Thought-Form Elementals

Water is probably the least used of elements for the purpose of forming thought-form elementals. It isn't that there is any reason *not* to create Water thought-forms, so much as that so many natural spirits of Water are generally agreeable that forming a Water thought-form is seldom called for.

Of course there are always exceptions.

The most common Water thought-forms would naturally be for Temple guardians. Natural Water spirits can easily be employed for this purpose and either represented by an object to which the spirit attaches or by some form of container with actual Water contained in it. However, a thought-form may be desirable for this purpose because not only is Water a 'wild' element which seems to either evaporate or seep away easily, but it is one which can turn nasty when contained for long periods of time and go stagnant. It can be tricky to keep a fresh Water spirit in captivity, and it somehow feels wrong to do so in a way which would not apply to Earth, which is stationary in general, to Air which circulates naturally, or even to Fire which is ever changing. Water needs refreshing.

Trying to maintain control over a Water thought-form of any kind can also be tricky. Try walking across a room with a glass of Water, full to the brim, and see how much control you are able to maintain. Even the most graceful person would be hard pressed to maintain every drop of Water without moving very, very carefully.

This should suffice as a warning for just how easy it would be for a Water thought-form to get out of control, yet another reason for their infrequency. Water can be contained, but it has a way of getting free, a little at a time sometimes. If it cannot get free at all, it turns bad. Hmm....

Water, by its nature, never seems to be entirely under human control. Even a small quantity which might be used in ritual holds a sense of the mysterious depths of all sources of Water. Creating a thought-form from a source which retains this mystery can be a real balancing trick. Then there are the associations which we have for Water spirits, many of which are malevolent. Like the Water dobbie which pretends to be helpful until it suddenly plunges its victim into the depths, many Water spirits hold something of themselves back and the magician who deals with them can never be entirely sure of their continued cooperation. A thought-form, which would not only be of this inconstant element, but would be created out of the deepest part of the magician's subconscious where our personal demons dwell, may just be a bit of a handful.

On the other hand, it may also be a source of ultimate Will and power. Never underestimate the power of Water. It can be used for hydropower with the same force that propels a tidal wave. In magic, the invasive qualities of Water can be put to good use by a competent magician. The spirit of Water can 'seep into' situations where another spirit may be prohibited entry.

With all that in mind, a decision to create a Water thought-form should begin with a very specific purpose in mind, and a divination of some form to determine whether the Water spirit that you create is going to decide to cooperate. A simple pendulum divination is sufficient, and very appropriate in the case of the thought-form as this form of divination is closely linked to the subconscious mind of the magician. This is one situation where it is appropriate to perform your own divination rather than to ask someone else. It is your mind which will create the thought-form, the information should therefore come from the same source.

Water thought-forms may be employed for many purposes, but of those most closely associated with Water the one that I would recommend avoiding is emotional love spells. Love spells of any kind are a bit dodgy, but even the Fire of passion would be preferable to the absolute despair that the unbounded depths of emotion can bring. Getting caught up in such a spell could overwhelm the practitioner, even if it was originally intended for someone else, and a thought-form can repeatedly rebound on the sender in never ending torture.

On the other hand, spells to calm the emotions can benefit from these same qualities. A cleansing spell performed on a place with use of a thought-form creates a natural guardian much as the Earth thought-form which helps in construction becomes guardian of the building (see *Spirits of the Earth*). Conjuring a Water thought-form for the purpose of accessing the subconscious can be very useful indeed, as it creates an entity with whom to consult directly. This is also true for thought-forms who assist with divinations or psychic acts. A thought-form to help you to attain general happiness can act as a 'guardian angel', or the really talented magician can create a thought-form which specifically exists to lull one into sleep. I would hesitate to conjure a thought-form to assist with dreaming though, as some things are meant to be accessed indirectly. An exception to this would be a temporary help with mastering lucid dreaming, i.e. learning to become aware that you are dreaming within the dream state which allows you to take control of the dream.

A Water thought-form may be appropriate for attaching to an object to represent Water in the same way that it might be appropriate as a Temple guardian. Any object which does not actually contain the element is potentially something in which a thought-form might suit.

Creating A Water Thought-Form Elemental

Ideally, creating a Water thought-form should be done in a ritual setting with plenty of pre-planning as is the case with the other elements. However, this element has potential for some spontaneity and there may be some situations where stirring up a thought-form out of a pond, or even a convenient puddle could be useful.

The matter still requires forethought, but with enough magical experience it is possible to work out what is required within a few minutes and the only ritual tool which is absolutely required is a bit of Water. In a crisis, such as a shipwreck, the subconscious mind becomes less potentially sinister as the survival instincts of the magician work at these deep levels. There simply isn't time for emotional demonizing when basic existence is at threat. The method in such a situation is not far different than in a more ordinary ritual context, although one might be inclined to skip much of the formal opening.

In ritual, the individual or group opens as usual and focuses all of their consciousness on the purpose at hand. On either the ritual Altar or a central location on the floor should be a container of Water from whence the thought-form will come.

The participant(s) will circle this container, deosil of course, chanting a spell (see appendix) and will literally 'stir up' the thought-form, utilizing spiral energies in a whirlpool effect. If the Water is on a table or Altar, it is beneficial to splash a bit of the Water in the direction one is walking to 'stir the pot' a bit.

As with the other elements, any sinister feeling which effects any participant would be reason to stop immediately. It is all too easy, particularly in a group, to 'stir up' something nasty from the subconscious of one of the participants which would immediately be out of control. This is to be avoided, even at the cost of the success of the spell. Another approach is always possible.

Once the participants feel that the entity is formed, it must be released. This followed by closing and banishing as in any ritual, and especially by grounding in a Water ritual. The dangers of residual spirits are minimal with Water, but the banishing is always a good idea anyway. The grounding is essential. Then, of course, the thought-form must be sustained.

Sustaining A Water Thought-Form

A Water thought-form is perhaps the easiest to sustain out of all of the elements. Water, the element of emotions and a carrier of electricity in its physical form, is prone to transference of energy charges with very little effort.

An object which represents Water can have its resident thought-form, and even some natural Water spirits, recharged through a simple act of touching a drop of Water to the object and projecting positive emotions at it.

As I have pointed out before, Water left unregarded can dissipate or go stagnant. For this reason, it is a good idea to recharge Water thought-forms on some sort of a regular basis, just to renew the connection to you. An item which is guarded by a thought-form and is used either in ritual or for a mundane purpose frequently is easily sustained by contact, but a Water thought-form which is sent out to perform a task may need a more formal renewal.

Naturally, some of the magic user's own energy will be put into this, but it is well worth the small expenditure not only because emotional energy is a cyclical entity which will actually come back to the originator in force, but also because the thought-form spirit is of the magic user's own spirit, and if left unregarded too long it could become malevolent and then seep back to the originator as negative energy which is closely attuned to one's own, causing depression or serious illness. In extreme cases, possibly even a form of possession by one's own darkest potential. This is not a nice thing to contemplate, much less to experience.

Water thought-forms, like others, can be reabsorbed on completion or abortion of their task. If this is anticipated, a good way to prepare for it is to include stepping into the source of Water during the original ritual to create the thought-form. Obviously, this requires a container large enough to accommodate the participant(s). Near the finish of performing the spell for reabsorption (see appendix), the participant(s) step into the original Water source and the energy is returned to its own source.

The Water thought-form which is intended to continue for a long period of time or indefinitely can be recharged through occasional repeats of part of the original spell of creation. The spiral conjuration would not be repeated as this would result in an additional thought-form, but a similar performance, a calling by name, and a phrase such as; "*I charge you* (name given to thought-form at creation) *with the spirit of emotion which I have given you to* (state original purpose), *and embrace you in my soul, that you may continue in your purpose*", would be added.

Water thought-forms are creatures of mystery and depth, much like natural Water spirits. Complete control of their eventual actions is unlikely, and in most cases I would recommend a reabsorption or a prepared evaporation of the spirit, which can be accomplished by simply making it a part of the original ritual. They are also creatures of emotion, which are something that can be unstable in all of us to some degree. Quite a lot of thought and planning should go into any decision to create such a creature. As mentioned earlier, I also recommend in the case of Water thought-forms, that one always has a look ahead through divination to see what one may expect from the eventual outcome, before one begins the operation.

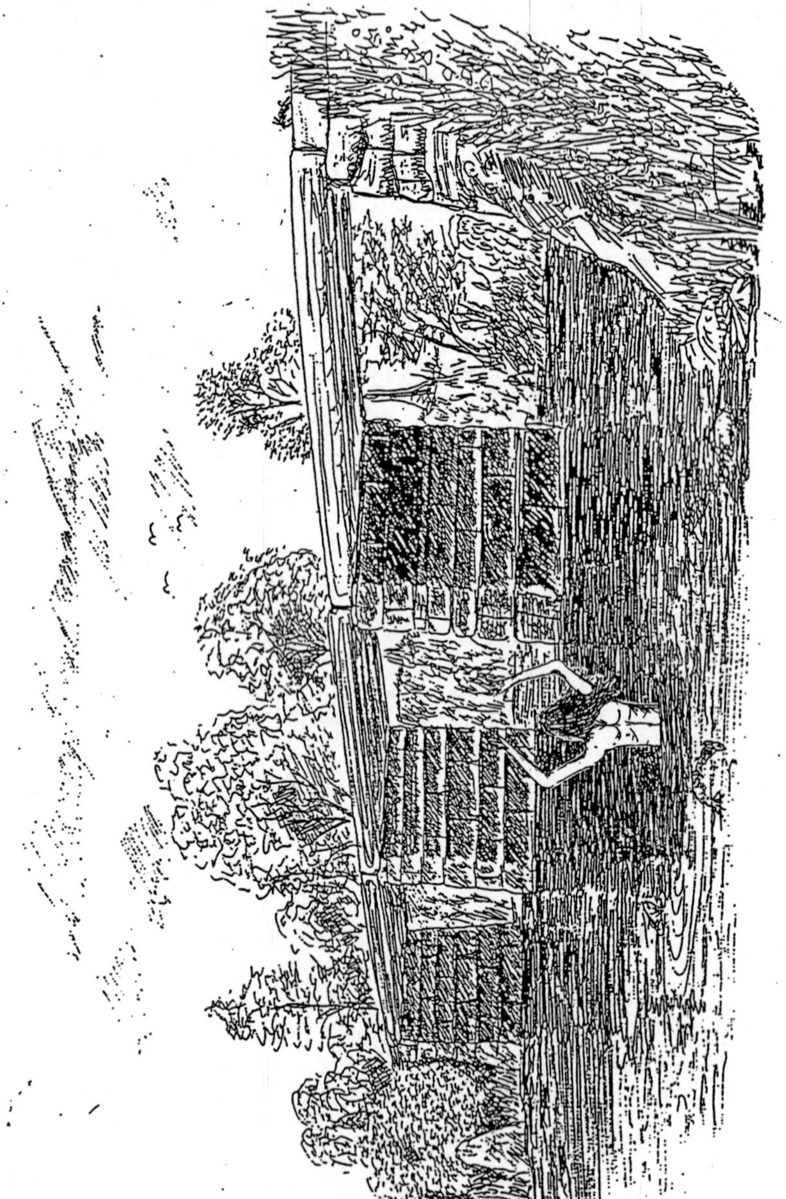

10

Divination With Water Spirits

The relationship of Water to the subconscious has obvious connotations in the subject of divination. In *Spirits of the Earth*, I explained that divination methods which involve material objects, such as cards, rune stones and scrying crystals, are associated with Earth, yet these methods also require the subconscious intuition of Water. In *Spirits of the Air*, I associated intuition itself with Air, but I was referring to the inspirational form of intuition which is associated with creativity. With Water, intuition comes from within the depths of the inner mind which still holds many mysteries, even to the world of science.

Naturally, forms of divination which are directly associated with Water will be not only those which involve the actual element of Water, but also those which rely heavily on this inner intuition. Intuitive methods of divination include scrying in mirrors, the sea, fog or heavy rain. Scrying by Water can be done through something as simple and natural as watching the reflection of the Full Moon on the ocean, a pond or another body of water. Some sources say that Nostradamus used a brass bowl filled with black ink, within which he focused his visions.

Dowsing is one of the better known forms of divination through Water. Although it is primarily known as a method for locating underground sources of Water, it is also a method

Wendy LeFay seeking images on the surface of a pond

which can be used for locating other objects or determining future events through selecting a choice from several possibilities. A variation of the traditional form of dowsing which uses two sticks or a forked Hazel branch involves using a pendulum to find objects or to make a choice. Many police departments in the United States have employed the help of dowsers who use a pendulum over a map to locate kidnapped children, although one would be hard pressed to find one to admit to it.

The sea has been said to "whisper messages" to some people. It is an old superstition that large one piece shells, particularly conch shells, held to the ear contain the sound of the ocean. The sounds one hears from these shells are explained away by scientists as the reverberating sound of the listener's own blood flow, yet the sound is uncannily like the sea and will sound loudest when the sea is rough. If one listens to this sound closely enough, it is possible to hear the sea 'speak to you' or in some cases, even to hear actual words within the rushing sounds.

The methods one chooses for divination are always a personal choice, but one should bear in mind that the methods associated with Water tend to be subjective. It is all too easy to see the visions you want, or hear the message you most desire to hear within these methods. Those who are new to divining, especially for themselves, would be well advised to begin with more Earthy methods such as cards and runes. While all divination forms are subject to misinterpretation to some degree, a method which provides physical symbols leaves less scope for manipulation than does a method which relies entirely on the psychic abilities and interpretations of the diviner.

Consulting Water spirits for methods of divination can help to add objectivity to one's interpretations. While the methods themselves may rely on impressions or 'whispers', these indicators can be made much more clear through the intervention of the Water spirit. The spirit can be beseeched to oversee the operation at the outset through a simple ritual much like those used in divinations for other elements (see appendix), or can become a part of the divination process itself. One may choose to ask the spirits of a source of Water to specifically provide visions or messages in another form, or to devise a divination method which relies on the behaviour of Water to determine the outcome or a choice.

As is explained earlier in this volume, Water spirits are often more forthcoming than those of other elements with the possible exception of Fire when it comes to divination, however, they are playful in their own way and may delight in shrouding information in enigmatic symbols or riddles in order to draw the diviner into their world of mystery. A Water spirit, when consulted in divination, will nearly always leave one feeling that there is some secret or more information which has not been revealed. This cloak of mystery over any information given can leave the diviner feeling suspicious, as if they are operating without the full picture and that some important but unknown factor may be essential to proceeding wisely, but usually the Water spirit will have given those details which are actually needed and may in fact only seem to be retaining additional information when indeed there is none. It's all part of the game.

Consulting Water Spirits For Spiritual Guidance

Water, as the element of the emotions, is an obvious choice within which one might seek guidance of a spiritual nature. The emotions are tied closely to the realm of Spirit, and all matters wherein one may wish some form of direction can potentially be well assisted by consulting a Water spirit. One should, however, be cautious about seeking guidance on closely personal and emotional issues through this medium as, although the element has direct associations with the relevant emotions, the Water spirits cannot help but draw one into the depths of inner conflict which may already be overwhelming at the outset.

The Water spirit which one chooses to consult may be a familiar spirit, even a thought-form, or the spirit of a body of Water. Many people throughout history have meditated at the edge of a pond or on the seaside, looking within the calming ripples or waves for the clarity of mind which would leave the mind receptive and able to address a dilemma or contemplate the relevant aspects of a choice to be made. In this sort of situation, calling the spirit of the source of Water to ask advice can be very beneficial and enlightening.

A similar consultation can be done with any source of Water. Filling a decorative chalice with tap Water and evoking the spirit within can be every bit as useful, if less dreamy and romantic, as consulting the spirit of a pond. Even a simple glass of Water would work in a pinch for a magician with enough experience to bypass much of the trappings of ritual.

One might choose to keep a container of Water specifically for divination purposes. The only drawback to this would be the need to change the Water on a regular basis to avoid stagnation. Otherwise, this would be an excellent medium. The problem can be overcome by using a black mirror which is washed before each use or by using a source of Water which is renewed in some way, such as an indoor fountain. A container of Water which is changed every morning as part of a daily ritual is also a method by which this medium might be maintained, assuming that divinations would be performed later in the day or at night. Of course this could be reversed if one prefers to perform divinations first thing in the morning, by changing the Water last thing at night. The idea is that the Water will have been assimilated into the energy field of

Figure A

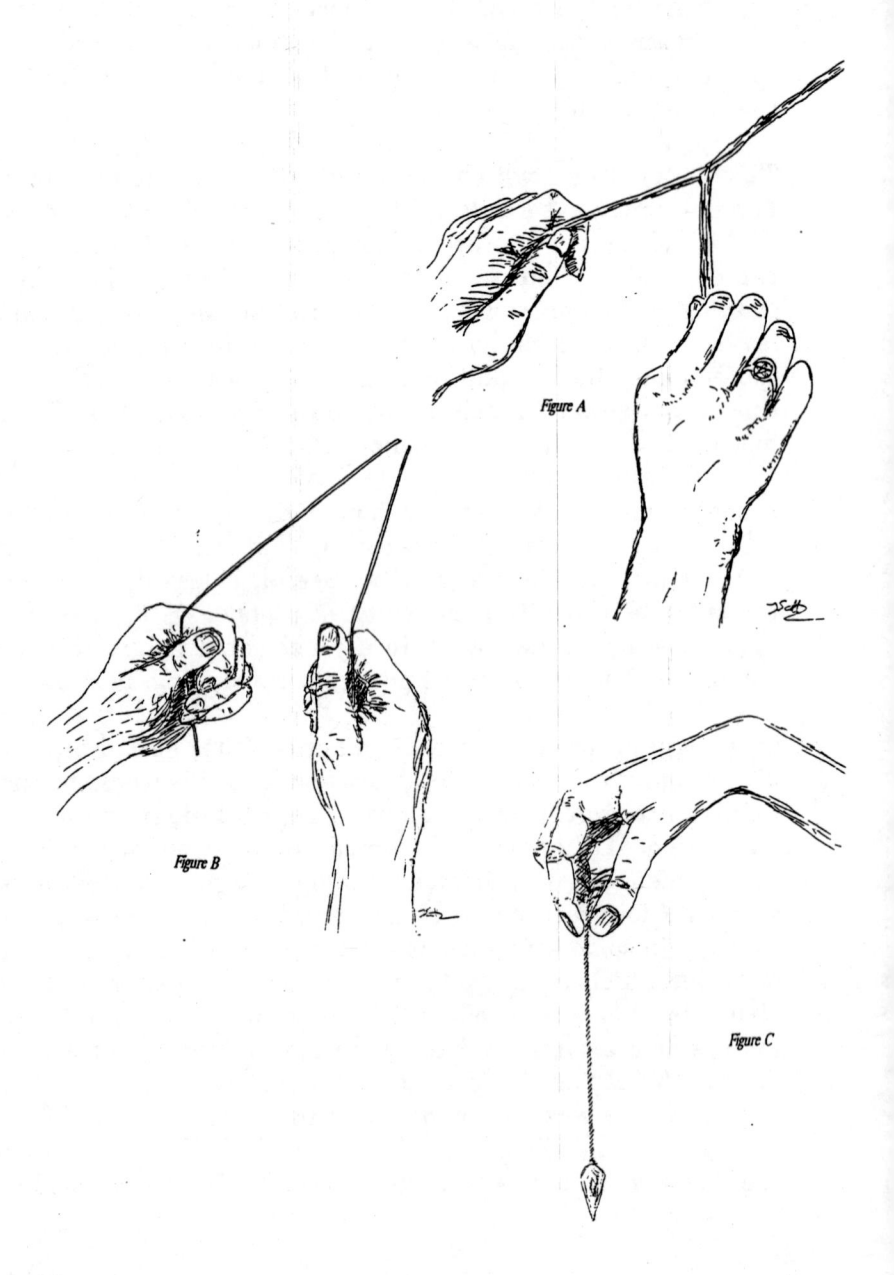

Figure B

Figure C

the ritual container for at least half a day before use, but is changed on a daily basis.

Methods Of Dowsing

The most reliable method of divining through Water is dowsing, as it employs a physical object which, correctly used, will direct the diviner in a clearly observed manner. As mentioned earlier, the most traditional form of dowsing is to use a forked Hazel twig to determine a source of Water. The dowsing rod is held with slight tension as shown in Figure 'A', and clues as to which direction to follow are determined through seemingly independent movements of the rod. A severe reaction over a specific spot indicates underground Water. Although Hazel is the traditional tree for making a dowsing rod, other trees are used and some people find that they are drawn to a specific type of tree for this purpose. I do strongly recommend respecting the tree and asking permission before hacking away at its branches.

A modern variation on this method is to use metal rods as pictured in Figure 'B'. Again, the rods are held in each hand and movements of the rods indicate significant areas. Both of these tools work on small movements of the hands which occur in response to subconscious impressions. Metal rods can be bought, but can also be easily made from wire hangers. When making your own dowsing rod, whether it is a tree branch or the metal version, it is always a good idea to protect sharp edges or smooth them over in some manner to avoid potential injury. Dowsing rods have been known to jump about wildly and eye injuries are all too possible.

Other things besides Water have been found through dowsing methods. As mentioned earlier, map dowsing can be used to find people, as well as animals or inanimate objects. Pendulum dowsing can be used either over an area of ground or over a map, as well as for asking questions in divination.

For the latter purpose, all one needs do is make a decision that one movement indicates 'yes' and another 'no', calm the mind and think of the question. Generally, either a North/South swing indicates 'yes' and a West/East swing no, or a swinging pendulum means 'yes' and a circular motion 'no'. This method is also known for determining the sex of an unborn child. The swinging pendulum indicates a boy while a circular motion indicates a girl.

Decisions as to these meanings are largely down to the dowser. It is the subconscious impressions which will answer the question. The pendulum simply gives the answer a physical form to read, which is easier to trust than an impression on its own. Like all forms of divination, one can suffer from interference if there is too much conscious effort or if there are distractions. Practice improves the ability to remain in a calm and receptive state, which is essential to this form of divination. If a reading seems to be chaotic and unclear, it is best to wait and try again at another time. Your focus should be on the dowsing instrument rather than on conscious thoughts of the process.

Like many forms of divination, dowsing works best when there is necessity rather than Will alone. Map dowsing can be used for a bit of treasure hunting, but this may be much more difficult than finding Water in the desert when there is genuine need. There are many different uses for dowsing, such as determining the best place to plant a tree or position a stone, or determining the validity of abstract concepts as well as the more often used purposes described above. Dowsing, like any method of divination associated with Water, is primarily a method for accessing the depths of one's own intuition.

Other Methods Of Divining With Water

There are many ways in which one might use the behaviour of Water to perform a divination in the way of simple folk magic. Most of them would be variations on two basic methods; either setting up a drop or stream of Water to choose among two or more possible paths, or dropping something into Water which can be observed for interpretable behaviour.

The possibilities for using drops of water to make a choice are fraught with technical complications. One may set up vertical, tightly strung coloured threads to represent choices and allow a drop, or a few drops of Water to flow downwards and eventually choose one thread, but this is likely to result in the drops seeping into the threads and refusing to flow beyond the point where the different threads diverge. Such a complication would suggest ill omen! Another variation would be to pour a small stream of Water down a flat surface, held at an angle, with separations near the end to indicate the assortment of possible outcomes. This is more likely to work from a technical point of view, but is perhaps too random to be considered a serious form of divination.

Dropping something, perhaps coloured oil, into a bowl of Water is a bit more useful, but again the oil is likely to dissipate into particles rather than forming shapes. Pouring the melted wax of a candle into the bowl of Water creates definite shapes, and might be considered as either a Fire or a Water divination method, which leaves open the possibility of calling "the spirits of Fire and Water" to assist in the divination, which can have a powerful effect.

Again, what defines a divination as being 'of Water' often lies in the degree of intuitive perception which is required, although the presence of a liquid is an obvious connection. My daughter provided a good example of basic Water divining a couple of years ago at a school fete. We came across a stall with the traditional string-bottle game, and, as she was feeling thirsty and adventurous at the same time, we decided to try an experiment in divination rather than taking the more logical step of walking over to the food van to buy a drink. There were two sides, one for children which had bottles of pop for prizes and one for adults where one could win a bottle of wine. We tried the children's side first. I paid the money and told Wendy to think of the element of Water, then choose a string which seemed to 'vibrate' with the element. She closed her eyes, touched her fingertips lightly across the strings, and chose one. It was a bottle of ginger beer, one of her favourites.

I can always tell when Wendy is successfully slipping into 'ritual mode', which she was doing quite noticeably during this operation (much to the bemusement of the volunteer mothers who were running the stall), so I asked if she could choose a string for me on the adult side as I quite fancied a bottle of wine and always liked to test Wendy's consistency when an opportunity arose. She chose the string, repeating the method exactly, and won a lovely bottle of peach wine for me. It would have been nice to try her a third time just to see what happened, but it's a small village and we had attracted quite enough attention with our 'experiment' already, so we left it with a prize each. I expect that we'll try again next time we come across the same game at a similar function, but wouldn't want to be indiscreet by repeating the performance very often in the same village.

In the depths of the subconscious mind lies many secrets and answers to mysteries that we haven't yet questioned. The spirits of the Water can help us to access much of this hidden knowledge through various divination methods as needed, but the closest and most direct route to these recondite realms leads us on a journey through the darkness of our most arcane selves. To seek the advice of spirits may shield us from some the worst effects of confronting the realm of shadow as well as providing access to realms beyond our inner knowledge, but none may entirely escape the emotional whirlpool of self-scrutiny in the course of even the most basic divination by methods which utilize the essence of Water. Behind the mystery lies ultimate truth, always a difficult realm for mere humans to confront. Water spirits, despite their fondness for mystery and secrets, can be our staunchest allies in the search for hidden knowledge, as well as for the realm of ultimate truth.

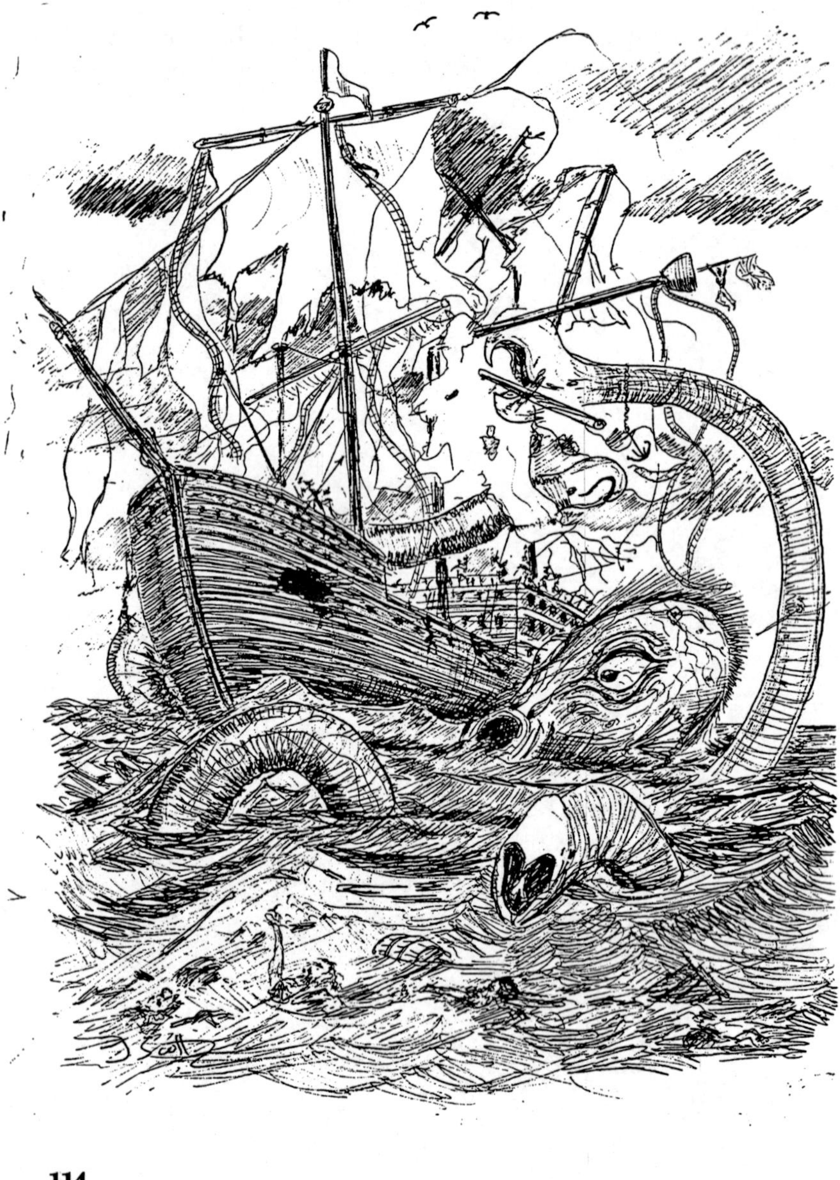

11

Living With Water Spirits

Water spirits affect our lives as constantly as do Air spirits. It is an element which is always present, always a part of us. This alone creates the imperative that we must work with them, rather than attempt to deny them.

Emotions are a natural part of the human psyche. Those who reject their own emotional natures, usually as a result of having suffered through some form of severe emotional pain or trauma, quickly become less human, less magical, and much more prone to some forms of madness.

When I was twelve years old, I listened to a profile of my astrological sign on one of those new age records which were produced in the '60's, and was impressed by one particular line, *"To be afraid, and not care that you are afraid, that is the courage of which Scorpio is made."* The line is a perfect illustration of working with the emotion of fear by recognizing it for what it is, yet allowing oneself to carry on and sort the situation in open awareness rather than permitting oneself to fall apart into a useless heap of chaotic emotion.

The concept can work with all of the emotions. The magician can apply the positive energies of love and passion to both life and magic, or the drive behind anger, or even the spiritual 'high' which accompanies the exhilaration of success or simple elation. While the stronger emotions require some parameters through the disciplines of magic in order to avoid getting totally out of control, all of the emotions have the capacity for being put to constructive use.

Water spirits, though they are potentially as destructive as the floods and tidal waves which demonstrate the pure force of Water, are also naturally calm creatures which can be as cooperative as the currents we create for ourselves when we go for a swim in a calm pool or a lake.

Despite the tendency of Water to entice one into its depths, it is an affectionate element. The Water spirits are sensual and intimate in the way that a friendly cat may show affection when it seems to attempt to 'become' a part of the human object of its attentions and to try to surround the larger human with its small but ever convoluting body. Water attracts in the form of sensual love which is the counterpart of death, yet the sensuality is never base or crude, the death in Water a clean and calm giving over to sensation and memory. Water is ever cleansing.

The gentle cleansing power of Water is very different from the more violent cleansing which comes from Fire, yet this could be easily forgotten by a victim of the tidal wave or flood who has experienced the full force of the power of Water. The nature of the element is reflected in the characteristics of the spirits of Water. They are inherently calm, yet are not to be trifled with. The slightest outside influence can change their gentle nature into a raging tempest. Tales tell of creatures of the Water who attack ships or entice swimmers to their deaths, as well as those who give freely of gifts and advice, or even magical favours.

This changeable nature attributed to the spirits of the Water is an illustration of our own emotional natures, which in turn reflects the mutable and sometimes unpredictable nature of magic in all of its forms. Change is a part of nature, as well as of us who are a part of nature even when we sometimes forget that this is so. Dealing with Water spirits requires an adaptability which obliges us to exercise some degree of command over our more turbulent emotions in accordance with our natural intuition.

It is the spirit of intuition which will lead us to the spirits of the Water, but it is down to us to learn the art of remaining in a calm frame of mind when dealing with them. We have the ability to allow ourselves to be drawn into the depths of the world of Water spirits without completely abandoning ourselves to their whims and mercies.

Friendly Water spirits may be the most valuable allies we can have in times of personal trouble. They can and will assist freely in divinations, spells to calm our own distracting emotions and all other purposes which are associated with Water. Perhaps most importantly, they can help us to open ourselves to the intuitive ability to see our way clearly through to the path which will take us where we want to go. Yet we must remember to approach with calm, and not despair, when we seek direction from the spirits of the Water.

Appendix

The following sample spells are meant to act as models and a beginning, but must be expanded and adapted to the inner depths of feeling of the practitioner of Water spells. Emotion is an essential attribute for this sort of magic, and much must be spontaneously created from intuition during the actual implementation of the spell.

The magic of Water works very much on the inner levels of intuition and the sub-conscious Will. Forming an emotional expression of a desire cannot be achieved simply by reading a spell from a book. It must be internalised, experienced in the inner being. These spells, as I said, are a beginning. It is by personalizing them and adding the appropriate details oneself that one may attract the attention of the spirits of the Water.

An Opening For A Water Spirit Ritual

A ritual which is specifically directed at the element of Water is fairly easy to set up. The traditional magical implement for Water is the chalice, usually filled with wine in a balanced ritual which includes mention of all the elements, but for a Water ritual I would recommend filling the chalice or some other vessel with Water, in order to have the actual element present. Alternatively, you may wish to immerse yourself in the element itself as described earlier in the chapters on natural magic and ritual. The source of the Water used in any form of Water ritual can be a natural source or something as common as your kitchen or bathroom tap, or you may prefer to use Water collected from a holy well or other significant source.

More than with any other element, Water is best approached in a state of relaxation. Beginning with relaxation and breathing exercises allows you to let yourself be drawn into the depths of the Water, which is essential to this form of ritual. You may wish to use your own wording, or to begin with something like;

"(I/we) *invite the spirits of the Water to join* (my/our) *ritual, and to bring the qualities of sensation and empathy with the spiritual to* (my/our) *purpose, immersing (me/us) in the spirit of Water even as Water immerses all and flows through every crevice of its path.*"

or;

"(I/we) *call upon the element of Water for this ritual for* (cleansing, fertility, love, insight, etc.) *and seek within the spirit of Water to bring the depth of intention and 'the knowing' to accomplish* (my/our) *purpose.*"

Calling A Water Quarter Guardian

The important thing to remember when summoning Water spirits for any purpose is to feel your summoning. How you refer to the spirit (undine, a name of a specific Water spirit or simply "*Spirits of the Water*" or "*west*"), is less important than the need to project the experience or essence of Water from the emotional depths of your own being.

Many traditions have their own traditional wording for this part of the ritual, but for those who practice independently or prefer to establish their own traditions, I can offer a simple example to work from as follows;

"(I/we) *call upon the spirits of the Water, of the streams and pools, and of the powerful oceans of our world, to witness (my/our) rites and to lend the qualities of intuition, of feeling and of conscience to* (my/our) *magic. Let the power of directed emotion bring productive fruition to what* (I/we) *do here today. Let it be so.*"

A Closing For A Water Spirit Ritual

As with the other elements, a Water ritual or the Water portion of a ritual using all of the elements is best closed in accordance with the opening, bringing the magic full circle. With Water, the participant(s) are likely to be in a very relaxed state at the finish of the ritual and having the finish very much like the opening is easier to cope with than trying to be freshly creative, so if a spontaneous opening has been used it is well to try to remember the wording as closely as possible. Following are wordings which reflect a finish for those which I have offered for possible openings;

"(I/we) *thank the spirits of the Water for joining* (my/our) *ritual, and for bringing the qualities of sensation and empathy to* (my/our) *purpose, for immersing* (me/us) *in the spirit of Water even as Water immerses all and flows through every crevice of its path. Let them now return to their realms in peace and tranquility, until next* (I/we) *require their assistance. Let it be so.*" (or "*so mote it be.*")

or;

"(I/we) *thank the spirits of the element of Water for this ritual for* (cleansing, fertility, love, insight, etc.) *and wish to remember the depth of intention and knowing that they have brought to* (my/our) *purpose.* (I/we) *release them now to return to their realms in peace and tranquility, until next* (I/we) *require their assistance. Let it be so.*" (or "*so mote it be.*")

or;

"(I/we) *thank the spirits of the Water, of the streams and pools, and of the powerful oceans of our world, for witnessing* (my/our) *rites and for lending the qualities of intuition, of feeling and of conscience to* (my/our) *magic. Let the power of directed emotion bring productive fruition to what* (I/we) *have done here today. Let it be so.*" (or "*so mote it be.*")

The Middle Bit

Whether the practice of opening and closing are a requirement in one's rituals or one is happy with performing the ritual without these formalities (as some would consider them), working with Water spirits lends itself easily to making a transitional period between the beginning and end of an act of magic. Water, as I have said before in this volume, draws one into itself. It is therefore a given that withdrawing from 'ritual mode' requires a similar transitional change in consciousness.

For this reason, most Water rituals can easily be approached directly, with or without formal openings and closings, but some people will always feel more comfortable using them and that is okay too. The following rituals can be done either way. I do, however, recommend some emphasis on grounding afterwards as the spirits of the Water are rather loath to release those who enter into their realms.

A Spell For Inviting Water Spirits Into The Home Or Temple

Those who collect this entire series may have noticed that *Spirits of the Fire* did not include a spell for inviting Fire spirits into the Temple as is the case with all of the other elements. Hopefully, the reason will be obvious. Inviting Fire into the home is asking for trouble. Similarly, Water has the potential for destruction in the form of floods and should be treated with reasonable caution, but Water spirits can certainly be safely invited in with a bit of forethought.

A good way to begin such a ritual is by cleaning the place into which the spirits are to be invited. Washing down the walls, even the ceiling, immediately associates the cleansing process with what you intend to do. You may wish to chant while doing this, something to the effect of; *"I cleanse this room of all negative energies and thoughts, and seek the purity of clean Water in all that is to be done here."* When this process is finished, the dirty Water should be poured away either down a sink or into the ground outside. If you are inviting Water spirits into a garden or other outdoor location, you may wish to similarly 'cleanse' the area by pouring Water over the space from a common garden Watering can.

When the cleaning is completed, the ritual is set up, including a source of Water. This may be anything from a small bowl to an elaborate chalice or a much larger container. It is a matter of personal preference and space availability. The ritual will be focused on this Water source, rather than on a candle or icon. The Water should be fresh and clean, although it is perfectly fine to draw it from a common tap. Note that it is not required for this sort of ritual to bless the Water with salt as in many ritual traditions, as the focus is specifically on the Water element. However, if you feel better doing so, feel free to 'purify' the Water in any way you wish.

An opening is performed in whatever manner you choose, then proceed with the invitation accordingly.

(for the garden):

"Spirits of the Water, who clean and nourish all that thrives and gives environment to all of the swimming creatures of the planet, I invite you join my garden, to moisten the roots of the

plants and quench the thirst of those creatures which dwell within this place and to make of it a magical place, wherein the realm of emotions may be balanced and employed wisely when appropriate, by the power of Earth, Air, Fire and Water, so shall it be."

(for an established body of Water, pond or pool):

"Spirits of the Water, who clean and nourish all that thrives and gives environment to all of the swimming creatures of the planet, I invite you to join my (pond, pool, etc.), *to embrace the lives of the creatures who live within your depths and to make of it a magical place, wherein the realm of emotions may be balanced and employed wisely when appropriate, by the power of Earth, Air, Fire and Water, so shall it be."*

This simple formula may be expanded as the magician desires. This is highly recommended in order to personalize the ritual to your specific place. This also holds with the following incantations.

(for the Temple):

Facing West as part of a ritual for all of the elements in turn; *"I call upon the spirits of the West, of the element of Water, and invite them to lend the qualities of balanced emotion to this Temple and all that will be done within it, to become a part of this place, and of those who practice within it. Let them provide the wisdom to know when the power of strong emotions shall be appropriate to the magic which is done here, and also to know when detachment from those emotions must prevail. Let it be so."*

A slight variation of this can be used as a house blessing as follows;

"I call upon the spirits of the element of Water, and invite them to lend the qualities of balanced emotion to this home, to become a part of this place, and of those who live and visit within it. Let the spirit of calm and balanced emotions prevail here. Let it be so."

Having looked at invitation spells close to home, we must also consider forms for spells to invite spirits of more wild or natural places to join our rituals. As is explained in the chapter on natural magic, it is important to remember that any invitation is being given to a spirit who is already resident in the place, and may well have been so for much longer than your own lifetime. To claim a place, such as a large lake or spot of ocean, and invite the resident Water spirits in, could be compared to breezing into a stranger's house and inviting them to join you for dinner. A bit of realistic consideration is in order.

The way round this awkward state of affairs is to combine asking permission to use their place with inviting them to join your ritual. An example of how to go about this is as follows;

"(I/we) come here to ask the spirits of the depths of this (lake/ocean/etc.) *to allow* (me/us) *to perform this magic in your realm of Water, and to join* (me/us) *in its purpose, which is to* (state purpose).

Then continue as with any other Water spell, but be sure to include thanks to the resident spirits in the closing. You may even wish to name a known spirit of the place in both opening and closing, but be sure to do your research first. Some established Water spirits, Poseidon/Neptune for the ocean for example, can be a rather powerful and independent entity to be calling up without good reason. Some lake spirits are known for claiming their sacrifice. Never assume that it doesn't apply just because there hasn't been a drowning in the last hundred years.

Inviting A Spirit Into An Object To Represent Water

Objects which are most frequently used to represent Water are a chalice or a shell, but other items may be used which have meaning to the magic user, particularly if they have come to you from a source of Water. Assuming that the item is intended for either an Altar item or to place in the West quarter of a room for general balance, the item is most likely to be a solid object of some sort. If, on the other hand, one wishes to keep a container of Water to represent the element, a simple vase which is kept partially full and has the Water changed on a regular basis can be very effective. If one is fortunate enough to live near a holy well or other special place of Water, the Water could be regularly ritually committed to the garden and replaced from the source. Still, it is the vase which provides a basis, as container, for the Water representation.

Any of the objects may be decorated either prior to or during the dedication ritual. As with any ritual, choose a time and place where you wont be interrupted and prepare for the ritual. The place may be the privacy of your own Temple, or you may want to do this one near or in a natural source of Water. It may even be done spontaneously, having found a particularly nice shell on the beach. Open the ritual in whatever way you choose, possibly simply by calling the spirit of a natural source of Water if it is appropriate to the situation, but as you do so, try to feel the depths of emotion enfolding yourself and the item in a special, emotional embrace which will bind you together almost as if you were a couple being bound in emotional (rather than physical) love. If appropriate, bath the item in Water and feel its texture within your hands, fondling it and making it a part of you. Then issue your invitation to the spirit which will inhabit it;

"*I call upon the element of Water, to bring forth a spirit to inhabit this* (chalice/shell/gift of the ocean or pond). *Let this spirit come willingly and without reservation, to become a part of the magic of this* (chalice/shell/gift of the ocean or pond), *and to dedicate its existence to the purpose for which it is intended."* You may want to state the purpose more specifically, but be sure that if you do so, it is forever more used only for the purpose as stated.

As with many rituals, the purpose may be infused into the item through a repeated chant, or you may feel that the dedication itself is sufficient. Close the ritual, and be sure to ground yourself, especially if the ritual has been performed in a natural source of Water. Refer to *Grounding After A Water Spell* at the end of this section.

To Charge An Object By Water

Water conducts an electromagnetic charge, and is therefore ideal for charging objects in many ritual practices. A very simple method for doing this is to prepare a large container of Water or choose a natural source, immerse the chosen item and stir deosil in an attempt to create a whirlpool. Actually forming a whirlpool can be very hard to accomplish from a physical point of view, but it can be done and it isn't strictly necessary for the purpose. The swirling motion of the Water will suffice. For maximum effect, have the container in a position where you may walk around it, not having to bend over too far to immerse the item, and circle it, also deosil, while chanting the purpose of the ritual. The deosil direction is appropriate to all purposes, even the most nefarious, as it reflects the natural movement of the Earth's energies. This is of course reversed in the Southern hemispheres. A simple chant may accompany the motion, perhaps a repetition of the intent or something as simple as *"I charge this* (item) *by Water, and release its magic to flow through the ways of the Aether to its ultimate destination."*

Some practicality must be considered when using this method. A sigil on paper or parchment will become soaked and ink may run. This can be incorporated as part of the ritual, running ink substituting for burning the sigil, or it may be that you will need to allow the item to dry before proceeding with the release of the energy. A stone or other solid object is unlikely to suffer any ill effects from Water, but be careful not to drop it during the process. This would seriously disrupt the 'flow'.

An item may also be 'annointed' with Water, perhaps from a sacred source or purified during the ritual. Again, the wetness would need to dry on a paper or cloth item which need be subsequently burned, but it would make no difference to an item which was to be buried instead to decompose over time. Releasing a spell can take many forms, and may involve any of the elements.

Evoking A Water Spirit Out Of The Depths

This may be something you would wish to do in the opening of a very powerful ritual, but be careful what you wish for! Water spirits of the depths have been known by such names as Poseidon, Neptune, Leviathan and even Nessie. Whether some of them are looked upon as gods or as god forms is a matter of personal belief, but they are very powerful images in any case and are often associated with destructive storms or disappearances into the depths. It is just as appropriate to use the method in local lakes, ponds or other sources of Water, but the most powerful aspect of the guardian spirit of the Water may well be just as potentially dangerous as the more widely known examples.

On that ominous note, the evokation is actually almost frighteningly simple. The only part which may require a bit of practice for some people is the act of projecting one's being into the source of Water sufficiently for the purpose. Obviously, this is only really appropriate to a natural source of Water. Invoking the most deep and powerful spiritual guardian of a bucket of Water freshly drawn and sitting in your living room just doesn't have the impact or the sense of ancient power which can be evoked from a dark pool or even a one hundred year old pond.

First, choose your source of Water. Unless you are extremely calm in a crisis and experienced in emergency banishings, take a magically experienced friend along to the chosen source, if only to monitor the situation and help with anything which may 'come up'. As much as it may be more effective to immerse oneself into the Water for this evokation, I would recommend that you sit or stand by the side of the source for this one. Water is treacherous at the best of times, and concentration on ritual doesn't mix well with Water safety even without consideration of potentially enveloping spirits which you are actively calling up. If your source is the sea, I recommend standing.

You may wish to set up an Altar and perform an opening, or you may wish to launch directly into the evokation as opening with the intent of imploring the Water spirit to perform some service for you. Do not do this without a specific reason! And always have a banishing ready, Water spirits can be very temperamental. Having chosen your place, position and choice of opening, begin by mentally projecting your being into the Water. Not the surface, but the deepest depths that you are able to visualize and beyond to the realm of sightless perception. Feel the Water around you, as if you were submerged within its comforting depths, embraced by its smooth and cleansing currents. This is the tricky bit... maintain a sense of grounding where you stand or sit while projecting yourself into the Water in this manner, and begin your evokation which may be something like;

"I call you, (name optional), spirit of the depths of (this pool, this lake, the sea, etc.), *to come to me from within your Watery depths, that I may ask of you assistance for my purpose."*

From this point, you may wish to state the purpose, or if there is no immediately detectable 'presense', you may wish to continue the evokation, continually imploring the spirit to come to your aid. It is important that you insist on the spirit coming to you, rather than giving in to any impulse to go to it, while also remembering that this is the spirit's place and that you are the intruder. It is also important to remember that Water spirits are known historically for demanding their sacrifices. Bringing along something to toss to the fishes, perhaps some specially baked bread or cake, is always a good idea. Also keep in mind that this is no time to go for a swim.

Once the spirit has manifested in some form, visible or not, it is likely to create a feeling of foreboding. This is not a task for the feint hearted. It should be immediately asked for the purpose intended, and some form of offering dispersed with perhaps additional offerings promised for later when the purpose is accomplished. Do not offer meat in any form, at any time.

Having made your request and offerings, begin closing by sending the creature back to its realm without personally banishing it which may go something like; *"Return now to the depths of your Watery realm and consider my purpose, until next we meet when I shall bring to you the promised offering."* Then immediately ground yourself, and banish any residual spirits. Leave the place immediately afterwards.

To Sustain A Water Spirit

Sustaining a Water spirit for a specific purpose, as with the other elements, is largely accomplished by repeated contact. However, a spirit which has been called from a specific source of Water may also be fairly easily re-evoked after a considerable amount of time if it is a constant Water source, such as a natural lake, pond or ocean. Water holds memory, just as the ever-changing drops of Water hold the form of the lake, pool or any other source of Water. Even the rushing Water of a river, constantly replenished with new Water, somehow holds the form of that specific body of Water. The boundaries may vary slightly over time, but the basic path or form remains much the same. All that is required to evoke a spirit of such a place is to basically repeat the original ritual, perhaps slightly changing the words to accommodate the fact that you are recalling a known spirit.

A Water spirit which has been dedicated to an object, such as a chalice, also remains constant, but is best given frequent 'drinks' of whatever is normally poured into the chalice lest the spirit dry up too far and become ineffective. A chalice which is used in frequent rituals, perhaps monthly during the Full Moon, is naturally provided for during these regular ritual practices. An object which is used less frequently may benefit from some sort of observance to maintain the contact with their element.

Something like a shell can benefit from regular ritual baths. All it takes is a few minutes to immerse the object in ordinary Water taken from the tap (although Water collected from a nearby natural source would be better), and to perform a simple observance. While bathing the object, quiet the mind and allow your consciousness to flow into the Water as in other Water rituals already described. Feel the presence of the spirit in the object, and speak words such as the following;

"(I/we) *commit this* (object) *to the element of Water, to cleanse it of all negative energies which it may encounter, and to renew the fresh and clear spirit of Water within its source.*"

More may be added according to your personal experience and interpretation of the object of course, but this covers the basic intent. Handle the object gently and kiss it reverently when removed from the Water, perhaps adding something like, "(I/we) *now return this* (object) *to its place of rest, until* (I/we) *shall again require the properties of the Water spirit which dwells within. Let it be so.*"

Simple Folk Spells And Other Magic

Folk spells involving the use of Water are many and varied throughout the cultures of the world, but the basic themes remain essentially constant. Water represents cleansing, purification, sustenance of a vital life force and perhaps most importantly, the portal to the 'otherworld'. The dark mysteries of the deep are a vital element in many Water spells.

Many spells will involve either washing or bathing something in Water, while others will require throwing something into the Watery realm. Still others depend on the magic user's ability to attune to the element itself or the spirit within, to use the medium of emotion to call the qualities (usually in their calming aspect) of Water into themselves. Any of the spells given in this series of books may be freely adapted to incorporate personal innovations, and the reader is strongly encouraged to do this in particular with Water spells.

Impromptu Water spells, performed on the spur of the moment and created from just a basic formula, can be very effective. The essential ingredient in any of these spells is to put oneself fully into it, on the emotional level, recognizing that the format of the spell only serves as a medium of expression and transmission for the channelling of internal or external spiritual energies.

Healing With Water Spirits

Naturally, any healing spell performed with Water spirits is likely to invoke the cleansing aspects of Water, to cleanse away the affliction. Obviously, care should be taken to assess the wisdom of using the actual element depending on the situation. An open wound may be either cleansed or infected through the use of Water. Fevers can be cooled or made worse with its use. Common sense must rule over any decisions taken on the actual use of Water.

However, calling the spirits of Water from a nearby source doesn't have to include pouring liquid on an unwitting patient. The spiritual cleansing may take place with or without actually getting wet. Actual spells would vary according to the actual illness or injury, but a basic formula might go like this;

Collect a large bowl of Water from a natural spring or other source, evoking the natural place spirit for assistance. The evokation may be worded something like, "*I call upon the spirits of this* (spring, river, pond, etc.) *in the cleansing aspect of Water, to come with me now and cleanse away the* (illness) *which afflicts my* (friend, daughter, husband, etc.), *and promise to bring back that which is not used or evaporated, that it may be purified through your own natural resources.*"

When naming the relationship of the patient to you, I recommend using 'friend' for anyone whom you do not know well or are not related to. The familiarity forms a closer bond between healer and patient, which can make a significant difference to the effectiveness of any healing. It is also good to name the person, 'my friend John' or 'my sister Sarah' or whatever is appropriate. This also applies to healing animals, although in some cases an appropriate god or goddess may seem more appropriate. For example, I recently performed a healing for a horse, evoking the aid of Epona, referring to the patient as 'your daughter Ebony'. I had, however, formed a bond with Ebony at the beginning, stroking her and 'tuning into' her as I would do with my cat, and thinking of her very much as my friend.

After collecting the Water, it must be transported to the patient, preferably without spilling it or speaking to anyone if possible. For the former, it may be practical to use a container with a cover, even transferring the Water to the bowl after transport if necessary. For the latter, if it is impossible to arrange in advance to get to the patient without speaking, keep any necessary communication as short and essential as possible, returning your thoughts to the job at hand immediately after speaking.

When all is prepared, proceed with a continuation of the spell which was spoken at the Water source. If practical, bath the wound or the forehead of the ill person or the afflicted area of the body, whatever is appropriate, with the Water while performing your incantation which may go something like, "*Let the spirits of the Water wash away this* (illness, infection, etc.) *and allow* (name) *to be whole again, to heal and become strong.*" You may wish to elaborate according to the nature of the affliction, adding a wish for an eventual outcome. For example, you may want to wish for someone with a leg injury to run freely and to swim again (remembering that you are dealing with Water spirits) or for someone with a debilitating illness to grow as strong as Poseidon or some other strong figure from mythology or a preferred pantheon. A short incantation can be repeated several times while bathing the appropriate area, or if using actual Water is inappropriate the bowl of Water can be kept close to the bedside and the spiritual essence evoked by a slight adaptation, such as "*I call the spirits of the* (river, spring, etc.) *to come forth from their Watery abode, and to cleanse* (name) *of this affliction...*" continuing with a detailed description of the problem and a wish for a specific result.

After the spell has been performed with the patient, the promise to return to the source must be kept. The remaining Water can be transported as it was brought, and then must be poured back to its source with thanks given to the Water spirits for their assistance. An offering should be left, as with any outdoor ritual.

A Fertility Spell

Fertility spells are most often associated with either Earth or Fire, yet Water can play a part in a more gentle form of fertility magic by way of Watering the planted seed in symbolic magic. This can be incorporated into a spell which encompasses all of the elements, or approached separately by someone who may want to avoid invoking Fire energies for whatever reason, which may happen spontaneously even in an Earth centred fertility spell.

A Water spell may also be appropriate in cases of artificial insemination, where the Fires of passion and the rebirth cycle of the Earth have both been bypassed by modern science, and the probability factor for the planted seed to quicken can use a magical push.

The most effective spells are of course those which encompass all of the elements, which will be covered more fully in *Spirits of the Aether*. For a Water fertility spell to have any effect, the essential components for fertilization must be present, whether through natural means or artificial. Specifically, for human reproduction, sperm must meet egg or for more agricultural fertility, seed must be planted in Earth. In Paganism of all sorts, the link between the two is strong and it is historically the act of human reproduction which is used to symbolise fertility for the benefit of crop growth. While this can easily be continued in modern times even with birth control methods in common use, it is well to remember that this practice comes from a time when producing children frequently was considered desirable, and that modern birth control methods can fail. Magic always rebounds on the user to some extent. If it is your garden that you want to fertilise and not your family which you wish to increase, using magic of any kind could be very risky.

However, if the intent is to produce offspring, a proper fertility spell performed in the fields may well be just what is needed to benefit from the reverse of the symbolism which our ancestors intended.

Whether in an open field or in the privacy of one's own home or Temple, the evokation of Water spirits in a fertility spell would take a form much like Watering your own private garden. As part of a spell which includes other elements, the Water portion would require a simple reference such as, "*May the Spirits of the Water bless and nourish the seed which is planted, that it may grow to fruition...*" continuing with a direction for a specific result such as, "*...and bringing forth the child* (or specifically son or daughter) *which (I/we) desire.*" or "*and bring forth an abundance of* (name crop), *for which (I/we) have planted the seed this day.*"

As a separate Water spell, using the symbolism of life evolving from the sea is very useful. Belief in this version of scientific theory is optional, as with anything in magic, the symbolism can be used separately from actual belief, whether it is in a god form, a theory of science or a concept of physics. This magical method was called "free belief" by Austin Osman Spare.

One way of employing the symbolism required for this purpose is to open a ritual according to your chosen methods near a body of Water which is appropriate for submersion, i.e. clean and of a temperature which isn't going to cause hypothermia. The prospective mother enters the Water, bathing freely and getting as wet as possible. The incantation to the Water spirits can be done by the woman herself, or performed by a priest, priestess or group by the Waterside. Incorporating the creative spiral energies is appropriate for this one, which can be done simply by the woman in question turning herself in a deosil direction within the Water as the ritual progresses. Ideally, she should have been 'fertilized' by the prospective father within a short time before the ritual, no more than twelve hours, and she should be at the most fertile part of her cycle if this can be determined.

The incantation itself may go something like this; *"From the depths of the Waters of creation,* (I/we) *call the spirits of the Water to witness the beginning of new life, of creation itself, as* (I/we) *seek to bring forth a child of the Water, a* (son or daughter) *sought through love and longing, and through the infinite power of the primordial sea do* (I/we) *seek the magical child which* (I/we) *desire this day."*

As the woman emerges from the Water, a group in particular may want to continue with a simple chant such as, *"Life from Water, creation to be, primal matter, life from the sea."* The chant doesn't have to carry a distinct message, but only abstract symbolism delivered through simple rhyme. Give the woman a large towel and close the ritual as desired.

A Water Meditation

Water is very conducive to meditation by its very nature and can be very useful in active as well as passive meditation. Passive meditation is that which is first taught in many Eastern philosophies. One sits in a comfortable position and clears the mind, a more difficult process than it sounds. Most people will find at first that the constant stream of internal dialogue interferes, as well as stray thoughts. With practice, one learns to push the internal thoughts away and return to focus, normally done either with a visual symbol in mind or a mantra, which is a repeated phrase.

A way of using the element of Water for passive meditation is to visualize moving Water, a river or gently crashing ocean, as a focal point. For some, it may be possible to focus on a still source of Water such as an imaginary pond. This is a bit more challenging, but can be done with a bit of practice.

An active meditation is one where some purpose is achieved through an internal action, such as a psychodrama where the source of Water actively cleanses something, possibly something which represents an aspect of one's life. For the more active imagination, Water may also take form in the mind to create things which one wishes to bring into one's life, perhaps in the form of a Water spout which delivers a representation of the desire into the meditator's visual field.

The possibilities for this meditation method are limited only by imagination. The key to success however, lies in first learning the passive meditation which allows the mind to begin from a place of clarity and calmness.

Charging A Driftwood Sigil

I mentioned in the chapter on natural magic that a sigil could be drawn on a piece of driftwood and returned to the sea as a spontaneous spell using natural materials to hand. There is some value in simply creating the symbol, carving it on the wood and managing to get the tide to take it out to sea, which in itself may take a bit of practice for those who are not familiar with the rhythms of ocean tides. Recognising when the tide is at ebb is important for the full effectiveness of this form of spell, and a bit debilitating to spontaneity if the tide happens to flow when the thought occurs. Much more important than the eventual fate of the piece of wood however, is the intensity of the magic put into the sigil construction and charging.

Some magical energy is created by the construction itself, as well as the act of carving out the symbol, which takes a bit more work than just drawing it (although this can also be done if you've gone out without a pocket knife, possibly by charcoal also washed up on the beach). More can be done through a charging. One form of doing this which can be done without drawing undue attention to oneself on a public beach is through an active meditation, as described above.

Construct your sigil on the driftwood and sit comfortably, closing the eyes and listening to the sounds of the crashing waves. Visualize them, but do not worry about accuracy. Allow yourself to drift into the ocean of your mind. Once you reach a state of calm non-distraction, visualize your desire being accomplished through some fantasy action of the ocean waves, being aware of the Water spirits which inhabit them.

If you are in a very public place, you may wish to stop there, but if you are away from people or unconcerned as to their curiosity, now would be a good time to petition the Water spirits for assistance with the task, which would have to be spontaneously worded on the spot to reflect the exact desire. Finish with an instruction to take this desire to the heart of whatever ocean deity you choose, and open your eyes. Throw the driftwood as far out to sea as possible, and walk away without looking back. Don't worry about its eventual destination. Ground yourself as described at the end of this section.

Cleansing and Purification Spells
Cleansing spells have an obvious connection with Water. The same basic symbolism can be applied to many situations and ritual formats, i.e. that of washing away something.

In a purification spell, the washing away applies to things like negative energies, distracting thoughts before a ritual, or some aspect of a person's life which makes them feel in some way 'unclean'. A spell can be constructed specifically for this purpose, or it can form the beginning of a ritual for another purpose, purifying the participant(s) in preparation.

In some traditional forms of magic, this occurs by the participant(s) having a bath before beginning the actual ritual, although the bath itself is considered to be ritualistic preparation. The main difference between this bath and any other is an internal attitude of serious preparation, although there is no harm in performing an appropriate ritual in the bath, perhaps pouring Water over one's head while saying something like; "*I call upon the spirits of the Water to cleanse me of all negativity and concerns of mundane matters as I prepare for the ritual to come.*" This same procedure could also form a specific cleansing or purification ritual, by mention of that which the participant wishes to wash away. The exact words would need to be specific to the purpose.

Within a ritual space, the pouring of Water over the head while intoning a spell for cleansing or purification is a very old practice which far predates the Christian baptisms which are well known for using this ritual formula. Again, the exact wording must be specific to the purpose, but the participant(s) may wish to begin with something like; "(I/we) *call upon the spirits of the Water to cleanse* (name) *and to wash away* (?), *sending these things into the Earth that they may be cleansed and purified through the natural process which cleanses all things. Let him/her arise now refreshed and renewed, freed forever from these things which s/he leaves behind. Let it be so*" (or "*so mote it be*").

A Spell To Seek Marriage

Be careful what you wish for. That is my first advice in this area of magic. Marriage or partnership with someone is too often perceived as a goal in itself, rather than a result of an already formed relationship which develops to this stage. If the seeker wishes to perform a ritual to result in marriage with a specific person already known, I strongly advise leaving magic out of it. Forcing a union in a relationship which isn't naturally developing that way is begging for unhappy results. Work on the relationship itself instead.

On the other hand, an unattached person who is seeking a partner may well benefit from a little magical 'push' toward meeting the right person, if it is done carefully and with forethought. The key is to avoid specifics and cast the net wide enough to be brought to the attention of someone who will bring happiness and fulfilment to your life, rather than to try to fit some unsuspecting person into a preconceived mould.

A Spell To Seek Happiness

Happiness can be a difficult thing to define, however, most people are aware of whether or not they are generally happy. Someone who is often miserable usually only has to look at the various aspects of their life to find the reason, but this is less commonly done than one may think. All too often, people muddle along in unfulfilling lives because of habits which they simply haven't bothered to question. This may include an unhappy relationship, an unfulfilling job, a lack of either a partner or employment, dissatisfaction with their current location, or many other more subtle aspects to current circumstances.

Obviously, a spell to bring general happiness must begin with a definition of what is needed to achieve this happiness. For this, the above Water Meditation is ideal. Set up a large, preferably clear glass bowl of freshly drawn Water. Place in the centre of the Water a single floating candle, preferably blue. You may wish to anoint the candle first with an oil which has a scent which you find calming.

Sit in a comfortable position, making sure that you don't cross legs or anything which may "go to sleep" during the ritual. You can decide for yourself whether to do this on the floor or with a chair and table for the bowl. Be sure that the bowl is close enough to reach, yet far enough that you wont light your hair on fire if your head sinks forward as you relax. Also, leave enough room around the bowl or table that you can walk around it comfortably as you will be circling the source of Water during the third stage of the ritual. You will want to begin with a passive meditation to clear the mind, followed by an active meditation to seek that which you desire. The third stage of the ritual will be to invoke the assistance of the Water spirits to achieve your newly defined goals. For both the first and second stages, you will also want to petition their assistance.

Begin with some form of relaxation exercise, then light the floating candle as you invoke the calming aspects of the Water spirits in the bowl. Settle into a comfortable position with palms facing upwards after lighting the candle. You can choose your own words, or use the following;

> *"Water spirits calm and deep,*
> *help me clear my mind to sleep,*
> *and in the depths of soul assess,*
> *my true desire for happiness."*

Clear the mind, allowing yourself to sink into a hypnotic-like state, but without actually falling asleep. This may take a few minutes or longer, don't try to rush yourself. When you feel that you have cleared your mind as far as you are able, proceed to the second stage. You may find it difficult to speak at this point, but clarity is not important. Focus on the bowl of Water, with eyes open or closed as you prefer, and ask the Water spirits to reflect your own desires back to you. Again, you can use your own words or the following;

*"Spirits of the Water now help me see,
my own true will and the path to find
to move forward to the goals which will satisfy me
and leave unhappiness of the past far behind."*

Continue to be aware of the Water element as you consciously examine the various aspects of your life, home, job, relationships, etc., and assess your satisfaction with each area of your life individually. Take your time and consciously work out what would be necessary for each aspect to make you happy, but try to remain realistic. Telling yourself that all your problems would end if you won the lottery won't get you very far, but working out a plan to get a job, ahead in a current job, or to start a business can be done with deeper insight into the vast possibilities that actually exist, but are so often overlooked. Wishing for an admired celebrity to drop into your life and become your partner is rather low on the probability factor scale, but examining how to either repair a current relationship or how to go about seeking a new one can easily set you on the right path now. Even little things like how to go about breaking bad habits or getting around to things you want to do but keep putting off can now be examined and planned out. The depths of Water is a thoughtful and insightful realm where the largest and smallest problems which plague us often become so easily resolved, if we are able to implement our own plans formulated in that realm.

Once all aspects of your life have been examined and plans made for changes, the third, activating stage of the ritual will help both your own resolve to implement plans and the positive energies which will help make things fall into place in the way that magic does.

When you feel that you have finished accessing all that needs changing, stand up with eyes open and address the candle flame, remaining aware that it floats in Water. Using your own words or those which follow, begin the first few words in your original position, then begin circling the bowl in a deosil direction slowly, gaining speed (in relation to available space) and allow the words to dissolve into a repeated chant.

> "Activate now my true desire
> Spirits of the Water, and of Fire
> Open the way and help me see
> Opportunities endless to me.
> [Activate now my true desire
> Spirits of the Water, and of Fire]
> (repeat last two lines)

When you feel that you have exhausted the repeated chant, stop in your original position and close the ritual by your chosen method.

A Spell To Bring Sleep

Everybody has the occasional sleepless night, but some have chronic insomnia or temporary difficulties over a period of time which cause sleeplessness.

Obviously the first thing to do in any of these cases is to try relaxation methods. Probably the best known of these comes to us from the practice of yoga. It is a matter of relaxing each part of the body in turn, beginning with the toes and travelling up until one ends with the head muscles, finishing up with the throat. There are two variations of the method. One is to tense each muscle and then consciously relax it. The other, which is often used in hypnosis techniques and I personally prefer, is to 'breath into' each muscle, intentionally allowing them to relax. Either method can be enhanced by using Water visualisations as described under Meditation.

Obviously, there are times when relaxation techniques alone will not quiet the internal dialogue which comes with things which play on our minds. At these times, something more is required. The best solution of course is to resolve the problem or make changes in one's life which will free the mind from whatever is causing distress, but this isn't always possible on short notice. The following spell may help, but the reader must remember that the difficulty must still be addressed by the light of day.

Place a bowl of freshly drawn Water next to your bed, preferably a fairly large, glass bowl on a night stand. Lie on your back and begin with one of the relaxing techniques described, including a Water visualisation. When you have completed this, petition the Water spirits to take you into the depths of sleep, speaking slowly and carefully. As you speak the words, visualise yourself sinking into whatever Water source was used during the relaxation exercise, going deeper and deeper into the realm of the subconscious. You may use your own words or those which follow, but use caution in the choice of words as you do not wish to be taken too deeply into sleep lest you fail to reawaken. A 'return clause' as is included in the following is highly recommended;

> "*Water spirits, take me deep*
> *Into your world where I might sleep*
> *Let my cares all drift away*
> *'Till my return by light of day.*
>
> *Deeper still we seek to rest*
> *Let mind be clear to seek it best*
> *In the depths of sleep and dreams*
> *Let all be well, go deep and dream.*"

Repeat the chant in internal dialogue, continuing to visualise your Watery descent and concentrating on steady, deep breathing. It may be necessary to repeat it a few times in difficult cases, always internally after the first time and with an awareness of the bowl of Water at your side.

On awaking in the morning, thanks should be given to the spirits of this bowl of Water, and perhaps some of the Water splashed in the face to break the spell and promote waking.

A Spell To Promote Lucid Dreaming

Lucid dreaming is what happens when you become aware that you are dreaming, and begin to take control of your dream, making things happen as you will them. Psychologists see this as a useful tool for dealing with inner conflicts which cause stressful dreams, which allows the sleeper to address the symbolic cause of the problem within the dream context. Often this takes the form of overcoming an opponent of some sort, the monster or bogeyman who represents the cause of the internal stress.

Dreams are very much a part of the world of emotions, and therefore the realm of Water spirits. A Water spirit spell to promote lucid dreaming could be combined with a sleep spell, or done separately for those who have no trouble sleeping. Either way, the spell I will suggest is very similar in form to the above sleep spell.

Place a bowl of freshly drawn Water next to your bed, again preferably a fairly large, glass bowl on a night stand. Lie on your back and begin relaxing techniques to help take you to the threshold of sleep. Include a Water visualisation with this. When you have completed this, petition the Water spirits to take you into the depths of sleep as described in the sleep spell, but using different words which are more appropriate to the intent, such as the following;

> "*In deep subconscious sleep and dreams*
> *Water spirits, help me see*
> *To be aware within my dream*
> *And walk the sleep paths consciously.*"

As in the sleep spell, repeat the chant in internal dialogue, continuing to visualise yourself sinking into a Watery source, but seek within your awareness of the bowl of Water at your side an awareness of yourself, that which constitutes the consciousness of you. Don't concentrate on this too hard though, or it may prevent sleep. It may be necessary to practice over a few nights to get the feel of the right amount of self-awareness. Like many things, lucid dreaming becomes easier with practice.

Don't forget that thanks should be given to the spirits of the bowl of Water on awakening, or petitions to try again the next night if you have not been successful. Elemental spirits should never be addressed in blame or anger, even though they may sometimes be slow to respond to our requests. It is not unusual for them to test us, to wait and see what we will do if they don't respond or to see if perhaps we might succeed without their interference. Too often we humans are quick to seek spiritual assistance and neglect to tap into the magical sources within ourselves, and spiritual helpers can become bored with this over dependent attitude which is interpreted as plain laziness.

Water Spirit Divinations and A Spell To Assist In Psychic Acts

There are many ways in which one might attempt to access the depths of the subconscious where psychic perception occurs. Techniques of scrying, automatic writing, directly accessing the Akashic records and so on are many and varied, but any of them may benefit from assistance from Water spirits.

The element of Water is of course closely associated with the subconscious. Water itself is used frequently as a scrying element. Just having a source of Water nearby while performing a spell, as in the previous two examples, easily effects the whole atmosphere of the working. Similarly, performing a psychic act in the vicinity of Water naturally inspires psychic energy and draws the level of the mind into the hidden realms. The obvious next step is to directly petition the spirits of the Water to assist in that which comes naturally, perhaps in some situations taking some precautions to avoid sinking too deeply.

First of all, choose a method for what it is that you want to do. It may be a meditative session, a divination or possibly even a direct scrying of a Water surface. It may be a spell which requires going into psychic perception. Choose a place to perform the act which is either near a natural source of Water or where you can produce one. Sitting in your living room with a large bowl of Water may be sufficient, or you may wish to perform your ritual next to a Waterfall, pond, river or beach. Admittedly, the natural sources are going to have a more profound effect for this. A bowl of Water is very much under the control of the practitioner, something which comes from the conscious mind, while a wild source is beyond that conscious control and can take us away into the deeper realms by their close proximity alone.

This is one situation, however, where I do not recommend immersing oneself into the Water, unless you are working with a partner or group and have someone in charge of monitoring the situation. The subconscious is closely linked to sleep and as one is drawn deeper and deeper into the altered state of psychic perception, it would be far too easy to continue to sink...literally. Don't forget the frequency of river and lake spirits who claim their drowned victims periodically.

Having set up your intent and location, one has only to petition the Water spirits and to proceed with the chosen method. Words from your own heart are always recommended and should be tailored to your specific intent and method, but the following example will suffice as a general guideline;

*"In depths of mind, to clearly see,
bring the images now to me.
Water spirits to me show
The things that I do wish to know."*

Not great poetry, but that's the point; it doesn't have to be. From a general opening like the above, the specific needs of the divination can be added in mediocre verse and will be just as effective as great poetry would be for the purpose. The important thing is that the words must reflect the emotions involved, the feeling of the intent. Then, having evoked the assistance of the Water spirits, carry on with whatever divination method you have chosen.

Spawning A Water Thought-Form Elemental

As is explained in Spirits of the Earth, thought-forms are potentially chaotic spirits which are best dealt with under very controlled conditions, most often created in an indoor Temple rather than a natural setting. There are exceptions to this generalization of course, but Water thought-forms can be twice as 'slippery' as any other sort, and I don't recommend calling up a Water thought-form from a natural source of Water to any but the most experienced magicians.

One would think that something spawned from one's own spirit would be relatively safe and easily controlled, but remember that Water is the realm of emotions...an area where few of us have much control at all. The internal discipline required to keep this creature focused on a specific intent rather than 'leaking' its way into mischief is no laughing matter.

Having dispensed with the dire warnings, a Water thought-form may be very useful for certain tasks, particularly for help in divination in a different way than the natural Water spirits which one may consult as explained above. Calling up a thought-form from the bowl of Water could provide the necessary objectivity which is required for subjective divination methods. Ironically, I suggest that collecting the Water from a natural source for this purpose is preferable to using tap Water. There is a stronger life force present in Water which is collected from ponds, rivers or the sea, which will actually form natural parameters from the act of being collected in a container. Tap Water is involved in a process of shifting from one place to another, and has a feeling of mobility to it as a result. Establishing containment is an important aspect of dealing with thought-forms of any kind, but especially with Water.

Having set up your Altar as desired and provided a container of Water, open your ritual in the way that you choose. The container of Water should be positioned so that you can easily walk round it. Creating a Water servitor is similar to those of the other elements; you walk deosil around the container as you state your intent and purpose, but interact with the Water by keeping your right hand (rather than a wand) just above the surface, allowing yourself to feel the transference of energies between yourself and the natural Water spirits who inhabit this Water. This is the same for those who are left handed, as to change would result in walking widdershins, which is definitely NOT recommended for this purpose. The spirit you are creating will be of yourself, but the natural elementals may choose to join in, or to get out of the way. Either way, the parameters of this thought-form will be unstable, so the more specific you are in giving instructions, the better. Don't forget to provide for reabsorption after the task is completed, this is important.

Begin as with any thought-form; "*I wish to create a servitor for the purpose of...*", then continue with the specific purpose such as, "*allowing me to see objectively as I read my tarot cards to determine whether I should* (specify intent of reading)." The purpose should be very specific, remembering that we are dealing with the realm of the subconscious and emotions. With a bit of imagination, the reader may see the potential for influencing any number of situations where subjectivity is involved, such as a job interview, but the ethics involved in deciding how far to go in influencing the opinions of other people is an immensely complicated issue in itself. I suggest leaning toward caution in this area. Such ethics exist to keep things from going very wrong.

Repeat your specific purpose as many times as it takes while continuing to circle your container of Water, until the feeling of built up energy is intense and you feel that it is time to release the thought-form to perform its purpose.

Releasing a Water thought-form requires an act of bringing it out of its element. An easy method for this is to suddenly change your motions while circling the container, using your left hand to pass your wand into the right which has been interacting with the Water and whipping little circles over the surface of the Water, visualizing the formation of a growing Water spout as you command the spirit to go forth and do its work, "*Go now spirit and perform this task* (specify task again) *and then return again to this place of Water, that we may blend again in harmony. Let it be so.*" Close the ritual and ground.

Obviously, you will want to save the container of Water for eventual reabsorption. Keep it safe from spillage. Once the purpose is fulfilled, reopen the ritual in the same way as before, using this same Water. Following the same formula as closely as possible, recreate the ritual but change your words slightly, "*I now recall the spirit which I have created for the purpose of...* (state purpose as exactly as before as possible) *to this source of Water. Let it now be reabsorbed into its source, and let it dissipate within my spirit with the calm of an undisturbed pond. Let it be so.*" It is rather effective to actually dip your hand into the Water at the point where you are saying, "*Let it now be reabsorbed into its source...*", thereby forming the connection which was separated in the previous ritual.

It should be very apparent by now that the purpose should have been thought out carefully before beginning, as anything which has been sent out is going to be reabsorbed very directly into one's own being. It is necessary to do this though. As I have explained, residual spirits are very chaotic and Water spirits are the most proficient for getting into things where you would rather they did not. Close the ritual as before, and do a very thorough grounding.

Grounding After A Water Spell

In *Spirits of the Earth*, I gave some methods for grounding which would also be very useful for grounding after Water spirit rituals, most notably both directly sending any residual energy after a ritual into the Earth, and lowering your internal energies by eating something sweet and with natural grain. Oats are ideal, which is a good excuse to indulge in home made flapjack, as it is made from oats and sweetened with honey.

The most important thing to remember when grounding after a Water ritual is to make the transition from Water to Earth, especially if you have been immersed in a natural source. When you have returned to land and have finished closing the ritual, direct all energy into the Earth, and include a transitional phrase in your grounding chant such as;

> "*From Water To Earth,*
> *I stand firm on the ground of my making,*
> *and ask the Earth (or Gaia) to cleanse my spirit*
> *of all disrupting energies,*
> *that I may be fully rooted to the ground*

*and Of the Earth.
Let it be so."*

Rest and feast, and for now, leave behind the Spirits of the Water.

Bibliography

Arrowsmith, Nancy. *A Field Guide to the Little People.* London: MacMillan London Ltd., 1977.

Bord, Janet & Colin. *Sacred Waters.* London: Granada Publishing Ltd., 1985.

Briggs, Katherine. *Abbey Lubbers, Banshees & Bogarts.* Harmondsworth: Kestrel Books, 1979.

Coghlan, Ronan. *Handbook of Fairies.* Berkshire: Capall Bann Publishing, 1998.

Froud, Brian, Alan Lee. *Faeries.* New York: Bantam Books, 1978.

Graves, Tom. *Dowsing.* London: Granada Publishing Ltd., 1980.

Heselton, Phillip. *Mirrors of Magic-Evoking the Spirit of the Dewponds.* Berkshire: Capall Bann Publishing, 1997.

Hughes, Ted. *River.* London: Faber and Faber Ltd., 1983.

Jones, Evan John with Doreen Valiente. *Witchcraft: A Tradition Renewed.* Robert Hale Ltd., 1990.

Moore, A.W. *The Folk-Lore of the Isle of Man.* Felinfach: Llanerch Publishers, 1994. (First published in 1891.)

Morris, Ruth and Frank. *Scottish Healing Wells.* Sandy: The Alethea Press, 1982.

Mullin, Kay. *Wondrous Land-The Faery Faith of Ireland.* Berkshire: Capall Bann Publishing, 1997.

Rattue, James. *The Living Stream; Holy Wells in Historical Context.* Woodbridge: The Boydell Press, 1995.

Sharp, Mick. *Holy Places of Celtic Britain.* London: Blandford, 1997.

Vinci, Leo. *Talismans, Amulets and Charms.* London: Regency Press, 1977.

Other Recommended Reading

Alexander, Marc. *British Folklore, Myths and Legends.* London: George Weidenfeld & Nicolson Ltd., 1982.

Briggs, Katherine M. *The Vanishing People.* London: B.T. Batsford Ltd., 1978.

De Valera, Sinead. *Fairy Tales of Ireland.* London: Four Square Books, 1967.

Evans-Wentz, W.Y. *The Fairy Faith in Celtic Countries.* New York: Citadel Press, 1990.

Foss, Michael. *Folktales of the British Isles.* London: GPS (Print) Ltd., 1977.

Gale, Jack. *Goddesses, Guardians & Groves-Awakening the Spirit of the Land.* Berkshire: Capall Bann Publishing, 1996.

Hestleton, Phillip. *Secret Places of the Goddess.* Berkshire: Capall Bann Publishing, 1996.

MacLellan, Gordon. *Talking to the Earth.* Berkshire: Capall Bann Publishing, 1996.

Potts, Marc. *The Mythology of the Mermaid and Her Kin.* Berkshire: Capall Bann Publishing, 2000.

Spence, Lewis. *British Fairy Origins.* Wellingborough: The Aquarian press, Ltd., 1946.

Index

Aether, 2, 18, 88, 126, 135, 156
Air, 2, 9, 13, 20, 28, 51-53, 55, 64, 74, 85, 92, 95, 103, 115, 123, 156
Alder, 18, 37, 51, 156
ALVEN, 19, 156
ASRAI, 20, 156
augurs 46, 156
Austin Osman Spare, 136, 156
Avalon, 32, 156
baptism, 35, 60, 156
BEAN-NIGHE, 19, 156
Black Dogs, 18, 156
CABYLL-USHTEY, 22, 156
chalice, 35, 43, 75, 78, 86, 107, 118, 122, 125-126, 130, 156
charm stones 37, 156
cleansing, 5, 9, 54-55, 67, 69-71, 73-74, 80, 97, 116, 119-120, 122, 128, 131-132, 139-140, 156
creation, 7, 10, 31, 88, 100, 137, 156
Dobbie, 23, 27, 96, 156
dowsing, 33, 103, 105, 109-110, 154, 156
dreaming, 0, 6, 69, 80, 97, 146-147, 156-157
Each-Uisge, 22-23, 156
Earth, 2, 5, 13, 32-33, 49, 52, 55-57, 60-62, 64, 71, 78, 83, 85, 87, 92, 95, 97, 103, 123, 126, 135, 140, 149, 152-153, 155-156

electromagnetic energy, 6, 80, 156
Faerie islands, 18-19, 156
Faery, 6, 9, 31, 154, 156
fairy, 2, 11, 15, 17-18, 21-22, 28, 32, 34, 36, 155-156
feminine, 6, 10, 15, 60, 75, 81, 87, 156
fertility, 0, 6, 33, 36, 69, 80, 84, 119-120, 135-136, 156
Fire, 2, 5, 13, 28, 49, 51, 74, 85, 92, 95, 97, 106, 111, 116, 121, 123, 135, 142, 144, 156
fish, 17-18, 21, 28, 47-48, 55, 156
free belief, 136, 156
GLASTIG, 22, 156
Glastonbury, 32, 35, 43, 54, 156
Great Source, 75, 78, 156
guardian, 29, 31, 51, 78, 97-98, 119, 127-128, 156
GWAGGED ANNWN, 20, 156
Hazel, 37, 46, 105, 109, 156
head cult, 33, 156
healing, 6, 12, 33, 35-37, 46-47, 69, 80, 88, 132, 154, 156
Holy Water, 35, 156
hydrolatry, 33, 156
James Rattue, 5, 34, 156
Kelpie, 18, 22-23, 156
labyrinth, 32, 84, 156
Lady of the Lake, 11, 17, 20-21, 32, 157
Leviathan, 18, 20, 127, 157

Logres, 32, 157
Loreleii, 15, 157
lucid dreaming, 0, 80, 97, 146-147, 157
madness, 9, 115
meditation, 7, 61, 67, 72, 137-139, 141-142, 144, 157
Mermaid, 7, 15, 18, 21, 53, 155, 157
MERROW, 21, 157
mirrors, 59, 103, 154, 157
Moon, 6-7, 13, 20, 60, 69, 71-73, 92, 103, 130, 157
Morgan, 15, 17, 21, 157
NEREIDES, 20, 157
NIXEN, 20, 157
Oak, 33, 37, 71, 157
offering, 27, 35-36, 46, 62, 64, 129, 134, 157
otherworld, 31-32, 52-53, 131, 157
pathworking, 85, 157
pendulum, 96, 105, 109-110, 157
psychic acts, 0, 6, 69, 80, 97, 147, 157
purification, 0, 5, 69, 80, 131, 139-140, 157
reflection, 31, 57, 60-63, 69, 72-73, 103, 157
sacrifice, 13, 29, 49, 59, 124, 157
Salmon, 17, 48, 88, 157
scrying, 59, 69, 103, 147-148, 157
sea magic 7 72, 157
seal women, 15, 49, 57, 157
SELKIES, 21, 157
serpents, 9, 157

servitor, 150, 157
shapeshifting, 85, 157
shells, 7, 19, 71, 75, 77, 105, 157
SHELLYCOAT, 19, 157
sigil, 69-70, 73, 81, 127, 138-139, 157
sleep, 6, 69-70, 80, 97, 142, 144-148, 157
Spirit, 2, 5, 9-13, 18-19, 22, 29, 31, 33, 35-36, 46, 48-49, 51-55, 59-63, 66-67, 69-70, 72, 74-75, 77-80, 83-85, 95-96, 100-101, 106-107, 117-120, 124-132, 146-147, 149-152, 154-155, 157
superstition, 36, 57, 59-60, 105, 157
swans, 17, 157
Tarbh-Uisge, 22, 157
Temple, 69, 77, 79, 95, 98, 121, 123, 125, 136, 149, 157
tides, 6-7, 71-72, 77, 138, 157
toad elementals, 18, 157
trance, 67, 70, 72-73, 157
treasure, 31, 110, 157
trout, 48, 157
URISK, 22, 157
Water horses, 18, 23, 157
WATER LEAPER, 22, 157
Water maidens, 17, 19, 157
WATER MEN, 20, 157
White lady, 18, 157

'The Spirits of ....' Series

"This really is a wonderful series of books.." Touchstone

Spirits of the Earth by Jaq D Hawkins
"It's all in here...really wonderful and useful stuff...I really couldn't put this excellent book down. I would thoroughly recommend this book" Touchstone
"A delight to read..a very highly informative and very readable book." Eastern Spirit
This is the first volume in the Spirits of the Earth series in which Jaq D Hawkins shares an understanding of the basic nature of elemental spirits with her readers. Within each volume, Ms. Hawkins explains to us the nature of the element, types of spirits associated with each element, and correspondences in magical thought as well as rituals and divination methods in natural magic. Included in *Spirits of the Earth* are the types of natural objects, and sometimes man-made objects, which attract Earth Spirit inhabitants as well as methods to see or communicate with these elemental spirits, places of worship or invocation, and the nature of thought form spirits associated with the Earth element. From fanciful fairies to guardian spirits of stone circles, Spirits of the Earth is a 'must have' for anyone who has an interest in elemental spirits.   ISBN 186163 002 6   £8.95

Spirits of the Air   by Jaq D Hawkins
"will certainly appeal to all those interested in Paganism and folklore" Prediction
In this second volume in the Spirits of Earth series, Ms. Hawkins progresses into the inspirational realm of Air elemental spirits and continues to relate these spirits to magical correspondences, rituals and divination methods. Included in Spirits of the Air are examples of types of Air spirits, methods for communicating and seeking cooperation from these spirits, expanded instructions for dealing with thought-form spirits and more. From spirits of storms to messengers of the gods themselves, Spirits of the Air is an integral sourcebook for seekers of elemental magic.   ISBN 186163 0654   £8.95

Spirits of the Fire   by Jaq D Hawkins
In this third volume of the Spirits of the Elements Series, we encounter yet a new perspective of elemental spirits - and find ourselves confronted with all of the passion and intensity, and even the dangers, of the element of Fire. Included in Spirits of the Fire are new aspects of the nature and types of elemental spirits as well as new approaches to elemental spirit magic. Also included are methods for focusing and directing the dynamic forces of Fire spirits, and for evoking the power of the spirit of Fire through ecstatic dance and other methods. Whether we seek the assistance of a spirit of a flame or the potency of the spirit of passion in magic, Spirits of the Fire is an essential addition to the library of any practitioner of elemental spirit magic.   ISBN 186163 076 X   **£8.95**

'Spirtis of the Aether' in Preparation

FREE DETAILED CATALOGUE

Capall Bann is owned and run by people actively involved in many of the areas in which we publish. A detailed illustrated catalogue is available on request, SAE or International Postal Coupon appreciated. **Titles can be ordered direct from Capall Bann, post free in the UK** (cheque or PO with order) or from good bookshops and specialist outlets.

Do contact us for details on the latest releases at: **Capall Bann Publishing, Freshfields, Chieveley, Berks, RG20 8TF.** Titles include:

A Breath Behind Time, Terri Hector
Angels and Goddesses - Celtic Christianity & Paganism, M. Howard
Arthur - The Legend Unveiled, C Johnson & E Lung
Astrology The Inner Eye - A Guide in Everyday Language, E Smith
Auguries and Omens - The Magical Lore of Birds, Yvonne Aburrow
Asyniur - Womens Mysteries in the Northern Tradition, S McGrath
Beginnings - Geomancy, Builder's Rites & Electional Astrology in the European Tradition, Nigel Pennick
Between Earth and Sky, Julia Day
Book of the Veil , Peter Paddon
Caer Sidhe - Celtic Astrology and Astronomy, Vol 1, Michael Bayley
Caer Sidhe - Celtic Astrology and Astronomy, Vol 2 M Bayley
Call of the Horned Piper, Nigel Jackson
Cat's Company, Ann Walker
Celtic Faery Shamanism, Catrin James
Celtic Faery Shamanism - The Wisdom of the Otherworld, Catrin James
Celtic Lore & Druidic Ritual, Rhiannon Ryall
Celtic Sacrifice - Pre Christian Ritual & Religion, Marion Pearce
Celtic Saints and the Glastonbury Zodiac, Mary Caine
Circle and the Square, Jack Gale
Compleat Vampyre - The Vampyre Shaman, Nigel Jackson
Creating Form From the Mist - The Wisdom of Women in Celtic Myth and Culture, Lynne Sinclair-Wood
Crystal Clear - A Guide to Quartz Crystal, Jennifer Dent
Crystal Doorways, Simon & Sue Lilly
Crossing the Borderlines - Guising, Masking & Ritual Animal Disguise in the European Tradition, Nigel Pennick
Dragons of the West, Nigel Pennick
Earth Dance - A Year of Pagan Rituals, Jan Brodie
Earth Harmony - Places of Power, Holiness & Healing, Nigel Pennick
Earth Magic, Margaret McArthur

Eildon Tree (The) Romany Language & Lore, Michael Hoadley
Enchanted Forest - The Magical Lore of Trees, Yvonne Aburrow
Eternal Priestess, Sage Weston
Eternally Yours Faithfully, Roy Radford & Evelyn Gregory
Everything You Always Wanted To Know About Your Body, But So Far
    Nobody's Been Able To Tell You, Chris Thomas & D Baker
Face of the Deep - Healing Body & Soul, Penny Allen
Fairies in the Irish Tradition, Molly Gowen
Familiars - Animal Powers of Britain, Anna Franklin
Fool's First Steps, (The) Chris Thomas
Forest Paths - Tree Divination, Brian Harrison, Ill. S. Rouse
From Past to Future Life, Dr Roger Webber
Gardening For Wildlife Ron Wilson
God Year, The, Nigel Pennick & Helen Field
Goddess on the Cross, Dr George Young
Goddess Year, The, Nigel Pennick & Helen Field
Goddesses, Guardians & Groves, Jack Gale
Handbook For Pagan Healers, Liz Joan
Handbook of Fairies, Ronan Coghlan
Healing Book, The, Chris Thomas and Diane Baker
Healing Homes, Jennifer Dent
Healing Journeys, Paul Williamson
Healing Stones, Sue Philips
Herb Craft - Shamanic & Ritual Use of Herbs, Lavender & Franklin
Hidden Heritage - Exploring Ancient Essex, Terry Johnson
Hub of the Wheel, Skytoucher
In Search of Herne the Hunter, Eric Fitch
Inner Celtia, Alan Richardson & David Annwn
Inner Mysteries of the Goths, Nigel Pennick
Inner Space Workbook - Develop Thru Tarot, C Summers & J Vayne
Intuitive Journey, Ann Walker Isis - African Queen, Akkadia Ford
Journey Home, The, Chris Thomas
Kecks, Keddles & Kesh - Celtic Lang & The Cog Almanac, Bayley
Language of the Psycards, Berenice
Legend of Robin Hood, The, Richard Rutherford-Moore
Lid Off the Cauldron, Patricia Crowther
Light From the Shadows - Modern Traditional Witchcraft, Gwyn
Living Tarot, Ann Walker
Lore of the Sacred Horse, Marion Davies
Lost Lands & Sunken Cities (2nd ed.), Nigel Pennick
Magic of Herbs - A Complete Home Herbal, Rhiannon Ryall
Magical Guardians - Exploring the Spirit and Nature of Trees, Philip Heselton
Magical History of the Horse, Janet Farrar & Virginia Russell
Magical Lore of Animals, Yvonne Aburrow
Magical Lore of Cats, Marion Davies
Magical Lore of Herbs, Marion Davies

Magick Without Peers, Ariadne Rainbird & David Rankine
Masks of Misrule - Horned God & His Cult in Europe, Nigel Jackson
Medicine For The Coming Age, Lisa Sand MD
Medium Rare - Reminiscences of a Clairvoyant, Muriel Renard
Menopausal Woman on the Run, Jaki da Costa
Mind Massage - 60 Creative Visualisations, Marlene Maundrill
Mirrors of Magic - Evoking the Spirit of the Dewponds, P Heselton
Moon Mysteries, Jan Brodie
Mysteries of the Runes, Michael Howard
Mystic Life of Animals, Ann Walker
New Celtic Oracle The, Nigel Pennick & Nigel Jackson
Oracle of Geomancy, Nigel Pennick
Pagan Feasts - Seasonal Food for the 8 Festivals, Franklin & Phillips
Patchwork of Magic - Living in a Pagan World, Julia Day
Pathworking - A Practical Book of Guided Meditations, Pete Jennings
Personal Power, Anna Franklin
Pickingill Papers - The Origins of Gardnerian Wicca, Bill Liddell
Pillars of Tubal Cain, Nigel Jackson
Places of Pilgrimage and Healing, Adrian Cooper
Practical Divining, Richard Foord
Practical Meditation, Steve Hounsome
Practical Spirituality, Steve Hounsome
Psychic Self Defence - Real Solutions, Jan Brodie
Real Fairies, David Tame
Reality - How It Works & Why It Mostly Doesn't, Rik Dent
Romany Tapestry, Michael Houghton
Runic Astrology, Nigel Pennick
Sacred Animals, Gordon MacLellan
Sacred Celtic Animals, Marion Davies, Ill. Simon Rouse
Sacred Dorset - On the Path of the Dragon, Peter Knight
Sacred Grove - The Mysteries of the Forest, Yvonne Aburrow
Sacred Geometry, Nigel Pennick
Sacred Nature, Ancient Wisdom & Modern Meanings, A Cooper
Sacred Ring - Pagan Origins of British Folk Festivals, M. Howard
Season of Sorcery - On Becoming a Wisewoman, Poppy Palin
Seasonal Magic - Diary of a Village Witch, Paddy Slade
Secret Places of the Goddess, Philip Heselton
Secret Signs & Sigils, Nigel Pennick
Self Enlightenment, Mayan O'Brien
Spirits of the Air, Jaq D Hawkins
Spirits of the Earth, Jaq D Hawkins
Spirits of the Earth, Jaq D Hawkins
Stony Gaze, Investigating Celtic Heads John Billingsley
Stumbling Through the Undergrowth, Mark Kirwan-Heyhoe
Subterranean Kingdom, The, revised 2nd ed, Nigel Pennick
Symbols of Ancient Gods, Rhiannon Ryall

161

Talking to the Earth, Gordon MacLellan
Taming the Wolf - Full Moon Meditations, Steve Hounsome
Teachings of the Wisewomen, Rhiannon Ryall
The Other Kingdoms Speak, Helena Hawley
Tree: Essence of Healing, Simon & Sue Lilly
Tree: Essence, Spirit & Teacher, Simon & Sue Lilly
Through the Veil, Peter Paddon
Torch and the Spear, Patrick Regan
Understanding Chaos Magic, Jaq D Hawkins
Vortex - The End of History, Mary Russell
Warp and Weft - In Search of the I-Ching, William de Fancourt
Warriors at the Edge of Time, Jan Fry
Water Witches, Tony Steele
Way of the Magus, Michael Howard
Weaving a Web of Magic, Rhiannon Ryall
West Country Wicca, Rhiannon Ryall
Wildwitch - The Craft of the Natural Psychic, Poppy Palin
Wildwood King , Philip Kane
Witches of Oz, Matthew & Julia Philips
Wondrous Land - The Faery Faith of Ireland by Dr Kay Mullin
Working With the Merlin, Geoff Hughes
Your Talking Pet, Ann Walker

FREE detailed catalogue and FREE 'Inspiration' magazine

Contact: Capall Bann Publishing, Freshfields, Chieveley, Berks, RG20 8TF